MEDIA MANUALS

Basic TV Staging

Second Edition

MEDIA MANUALS

Basic
TV
Staging

Second Edition

Gerald
Millerson

Focal Press · London & Boston

Focal Press
is an imprint of the Butterworth Group
which has principal offices in
London, Sydney, Toronto, Wellington, Durban and Boston.

First edition 1974
Reprinted 1979
Second edition 1982

© Butterworth & Co (Publishers) Ltd, 1982

British Library Cataloguing in Publication Data

Millerson, Gerald
Basic TV Staging./2nd ed./(Media Manuals)
1. Television programs
2. Television — stage-setting and scenery
I. Title II. Series
791.45'025   PN1992.8.S7
ISBN 0-240-51191-3

Printed in Great Britain by A. Wheaton & Co. Ltd., Exeter

Contents

Introduction

This book provides for you in a single volume, a survey of the basic design mechanics of TV STAGING.

The student of the art will find here examples of all the main techniques and structures used in TV studio staging, together with indications of the flexibility and pictorial opportunity they offer.

This book is essentially an 'anatomy' of the set designer's techniques. The individual creative artist will, through the use of these mechanics, express his own personal treatments. These are the tools, the mechanisms at his disposal.

This source-book will serve, too, as a reminder of alternative techniques, to trigger fresh ideas and approaches and to encourage style variations.

For those designing staging for small TV studios, we include here details of simple, economic, but highly effective methods that allow variety and individuality in presentation.

The design mechanics included in this book do, of course, have much wider fields of application than the TV or motion picture studio. All three-dimensional display techniques in window dressing, exhibition work, museum presentation, and similar areas of visual persuasion, can draw upon them to great advantage.

Finally, for the more general reader, there is the pleasure of knowing how effects may be achieved. And this in turn can add to his appreciation of the media.

Acknowledgements

The author would like to thank the Director of Engineering of the British Broadcasting Corporation for permission to publish this book. He would also like to express his appreciation of the help of his colleague, Mr. Stephen Bundy, former Head of Scenic Design, BBC TV Service, for many years a widely experienced and esteemed designer, who very kindly examined this manuscript.

The Purpose of Staging

Whenever we deliberately arrange or contrive a scene in front of the camera, we are, strictly speaking, controlling the *staging*.

Fundamentally, staging aims to modify, to augment, or to create a particular pictorial effect. Through the persuasive skills of staging, we create reality, or conjure that which never was. We give plausibility to the unlikely or make the impossible a fact. Staging is a transitory world of make-believe, where the fantastic and the imaginary are given substance, where for a brief while we build an illusion.

On location and in studio

Away from the TV studios, *on location* (for a filmed or mobile video-taped sequence), staging often necessitates the alteration of an existing situation. Furniture needs to be rearranged, extra scenic elements introduced, or selected features disguised or obliterated to suit the camera viewpoint.

Within the TV studio, staging invariably involves building some form of structured background which is then systematically lit by the lighting director. Whether this setting (set, scenery) is of unsophisticated or complex design is not itself important. It is the effectiveness of the visual presentation that counts.

Background influences

At its simplest, staging provides a *background* to performers. Even the plainest surface has a direct influence on the audience impact of the picture. We have only to compare the diverse effects of dazzling scarlet and sombre grey backgrounds, to realise how important the setting is to the presentation. If wrongly chosen, a background may dominate, distract, or have quite unsuitable associations. But if well selected, our subject is given appropriate prominence, and attention is suitably directed within the picture.

Diversity of staging

Staging can explore an exciting range of pictorial opportunities. One can fabricate an environment, perhaps devising a replica so convincing as to stand even close-range scrutiny by the camera. Staging may lay emphasis instead upon decorative display to establish an atmospheric effect or a mood. By skilful staging, lighting and cameracraft (and the three essentials go hand in hand), we can direct the audience's emotions, and their interpretation of the picture.

Staging is a broadly based craft, and the good designer is not only a creative artist, but a resourceful craftsman whose feet are firmly on the ground. He works with an understanding of the allied studio operations contributing to the total production, with a wary eye on the economic and safety factors involved.

THE PURPOSE OF STAGING

Backgrounds
Staging may simply serve as a neutral background to a subject.

Environment
Staging can suggest a particular environment, or create an atmospheric effect.

Emphasis
Staging can enhance a subject, stressing its importance. Or it may distract attention from a subject.

Distraction
Staging may confuse, and make the subject difficult to discern.

Staging Meets Many Requirements

Staging is the fabric of illusion. But it must above all things follow very practical lines.

Staging should be appropriately *budgeted*. Costs have to be assessed, not in terms of money alone, but of available work effort (man hours, time schedules, materials, space, facilities, storage, transportation, etc.), and in conjunction with other facility usage or other productional requirements.

Staging must be organised within the studio parameters. Studio dimensions govern the maximum area and height of settings (page 14).

Productional mechanics

Staging needs to provide optimum shot opportunity for cameras to enable smooth, effective production techniques (page 86) to take place. Many TV directors, having indicated their broad requirements, leave staging and lighting details to the respective specialists, devising their shots within this total scene. Some analyse their intended camera treatment as specific pictorial arrangements, and the set designer provides staging to fit these shots.

Staging should take into account the technical and artistic problems that arise from studio mechanics and operations, the limited TV picture size, and the performance characteristics of the TV camera.

Camera lens angles modify the viewer's impression of size, proportion and perspective. A wide angle lens (short focal length) exaggerates distance and spatial illusion, while a narrow angle lens (long focal length) seemingly contracts and compresses space and depth. These idiosyncracies can be turned to advantage.

Staging must be designed with *lighting* requirements in mind. A specialist craft, lighting treatment can be impeded or frustrated by inept staging (pages 16, 18).

Sound pick-up requirements must similarly be considered in staging design (page 160).

Safety considerations

Safety considerations are a principal concern in all staging. The aspects needing care are diverse: firm, stable construction; suitable weight distribution and loading; fireproofed scenery and dressings; no unguarded stairs or high points; non-slip floor surfaces; no precariously balanced furniture or properties; no sharp-edged or spiked projections; no easily shattered materials (e.g. glass windows); no materials liable to explode or give off noxious fumes; no hazards of fire, gas, water, steam . . . The list is long, so long that for network studios the required precautions fill substantial safety manuals. But even workers in small studios would do well to be wary of potential dangers.

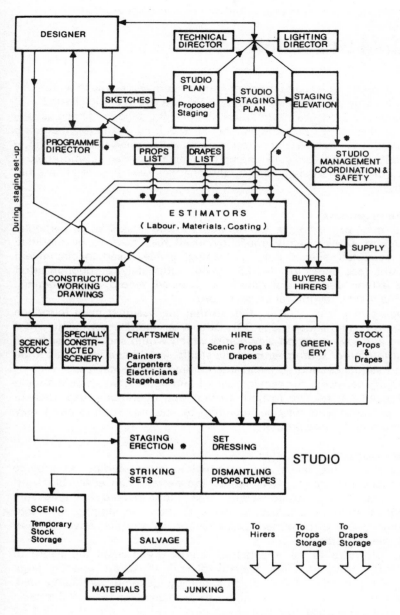

❀ reference back to designer

SCENIC ORGANISATION

Designer's work

A typical work-flow pattern for the set designer. Many important associations
have been omitted for simplification (e.g. graphics, special effects, costume
design, etc.).

13

Studio Utilisation

Staging techniques can be directly influenced by the way in which the show is to be produced. Presentation may be *live* (i.e. transmitted as it happens), devised as a *continuous recording* (i.e. taped or filmed usually with retakes of faulty sections), or derived from an *edited recording* (i.e. shot in any convenient order, perhaps with multi-versions, and later edited into its final form). In staging for a live performance, smooth continuity of operations is essential, any changes being made rapidly but quietly.

Space problems
Space may prove to be too limited for the needs of a particular production. Consequently, the show itself may have to be modified (e.g. rescripted, scenes cut), or staging devices used to circumvent problems (see pages 70, 74, 76, 80-84). Ultimately, production effort could extend over several days (i.e. rehearse, record, strike staging; erect new sets, relight, rehearse, record).

Staging height is often limited, so that the designer must introduce means to restrict shots (page 88). Otherwise, the director has to avoid distant and low elevation viewpoints which would shoot past scenery.

Distribution of settings around the studio should enable scenes to be shot in sequence, and so avoid intertwining camera cables.

Equipment access for camera, sound and lighting equipment should be allowed for, relative to both storage and operational use. Camera shots or movements may be frustrated by staging. Sound booms may lack room to operate properly.

Precautions
Safety ways (fire lanes) are essential in most studios, to provide access and exit points. Cycloramas and flattage can easily block off large areas of the studio setting area. Floor-marked fire lanes are obligatory round the edges of many studios, no staging or stored equipment being permitted there. Floor cables are covered with 'walk-over' boards.

Hazards have to be anticipated. Larger TV studios are liable to problems arising from the diversity of staff in action, and the large work effort needed. Small studios quickly become very congested, cable strewn, have critical storage-area problems and restricted access. These, like the positioning of 'dead' and 'live' scenic packs, must be anticipated in the designer's planning. Care is essential everywhere, to avoid the risks of fire, and electric shocks (ground/earth all electrical equipment) and problems with water, floor slippage, visibility behind sets (where staging cuts off light), ladder and cable storage, temporary scenic storage (of struck, standby and waiting items), safety slings for hung equipment, etc. . . . (pages 12, 26, 144).

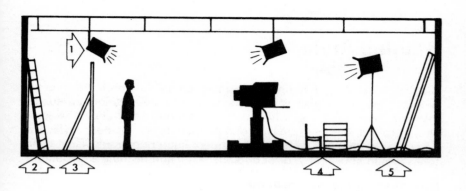

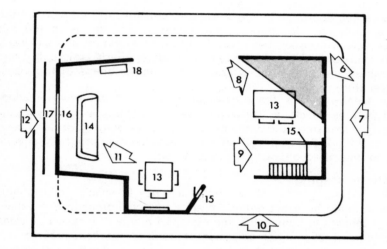

STUDIO UTILISATION

Staging hazards
1. Staging height may be limited by the maximum height of studio lamps.
2. Steps (ladders or treads) should not be in the safety way. 3. Scenic braces can obstruct free movement and access. 4. Furniture and properties may become littered around the studio floor, so some arrangements should be made for adequate storage space. 5. Cables for lighting, cameras, etc., need 'walkover' boards to prevent tripping people up.

Staging shortcomings and solutions
6. The setting should not be too close to the cyclorama. 7. Safety lights needed in potentially dark areas in the studio (i.e. those obscured from set lighting). 8. A larger ceiling than necessary may cause unduly restricting lighting. 9. Narrow staging area can be improved with a hinged flat. 10. There should be fire exits or access to staging round most of setting area. 11. Settings should not be too close together, leaving insufficient room for their respective cameras, booms, etc. 12. Scenic backing against studio wall prevents proper wall access (for power, camera, sound/light plugging points).
Key: 13, Tables; 14, Couch; 15, Door; 16, Window; 17, Backing; 18, Fireplace.

15

Staging Style

Staging style should normally be matched to suit both the type of programme material and its particular approach presentation. Where, for instance, the show is whimsical or tongue-in-the-cheek, staging should reflect this with an appropriately amusing, off-beat style. But where the production is seriously slanted, such humorous visual over-tones would appear coy, or of dubious taste, and become a distraction.

Non-associative backgrounds
The simplest staging of all is the plain, black background (page 110). This *cameo* approach isolates and concentrates attention on lighter-toned subjects. But dark or shadowed subject areas merge into blackness. Moreover, the overall low-toned effect becomes tiring to watch for long. White limbo backgrounds similarly isolate, but lack sustained visual appeal, dazzle, and cause subjects to reproduce darker than usual.

From tonal extremes, the concept of *neutral*, and non-representational backgrounds develops. These provide an unobtrusive setting for the subject, conveying no definite associative ideas of time, locale or mood (pages 110, 112). Such self-effacing neutrality may prove effective, or dull to watch, according to its application.

Realistic staging
Realistic staging may follow any of a series of styles. Some staging aims at being an exact *replica* of an actual environment. But usually, one is seeking to convey the impression of a type of location—a sleazy bar, an hotel foyer, a rich apartment through *atmospheric realism*.

A more sophisticated style makes no attempt at direct environmental imitation. Instead, by selecting readily associated details from a typical location, it relies on *symbolic realism*. A few scenic elements suggest, remind, imply, rather than imitate. Thus, a leafy branch (or even its shadow) can convey an open-air scene, a nearby tree, springtime.

Decorative staging
Sometimes emphasis is upon decorative pattern—upon the *abstract* use of shape, form, texture, and colour to please the eye, usually without direct realistic allusions.

Staging may occasionally take *bizarre* forms, which deliberately caricature reality and produce distortions that can equally well amuse or terrify as the contorted images mirror the world about us. Such fantasy can range from the nightmare ugliness of misshapen construc-tions, to evocative staging in which selected furniture and scenic units tantalise our imagination into an illusion of space.

Fantasy can concentrate instead on *silhouette* outlines. And certain skeletal staging techniques make intriguing use of this decorative effect (page 78).

STAGING STYLE

Neutral backgrounds
The simplest staging uses a plain background. Neutral backgrounds are
essentially non-associative.

Realistic staging
Can take the form of : Replicas directly imitating a specific place ; Atmospheric
realism, capturing the spirit of a type of location ; Symbolic realism, implying an
idea, usually through selective presentation.

Fantasy
Consists of : The abstract, a design without direct realistic allusions ; The bizarre,
strangely distorted for fear or fun ; The silhouette, achieving decorative effect
by concentrating on outline.

Staging Opportunities

A number of factors must always intervene between the sketch pad and the televised picture, and we must recognise these from the outset.

Design parameters

Most obvious, are the *inherent physical parameters*, e.g. the budget, time, space and work effort possible. Constructional mechanics production treatments, all influence potential design aspirations.

Less tangible, is the effect of 'audience prejudice'. Staging often needs to conform with established concepts, to be accepted as 'authentic'. A recognised—even caricatured—version of an environment, may seem more realistic to the audience than an accurately interpreted, but untypical or unfamiliar version.

Design interpretation itself can be a very individual matter. One can often stage a given show in a diversity of ways.

The inherent nature of a show often dictates presentational methods. Talks, quizzes, piano recitals, televised throughout world TV, take remarkably similar forms. This is partly a matter of established convention, but primarily the result of rationalised production treatment. They are that way, because that treatment gets the best results, or gives the best production opportunities. If one uses quite different ways to present the subjects, the chances are that shot incongruities, or some other operational problem will arise, or mechanics become over-complicated.

The set designer's task is, nevertheless, to keep recurrent presentations looking fresh, interesting, eye-catching, and appropriate to the needs of the individual show.

Basic categories

Most TV staging falls into recognisable basic categories which include:

Area staging. For large area demonstrations (e.g. dance routines). Frequently using scenic units (e.g. free standing or hung; rostra) in front of an open cyc. (open sets).

Table set-ups. Discussion groups around/along tables. Demonstrations at tables.

Audience shows. Studio audience on integral raked seating, watching theatrical-type open staging (action before backdrop or tabs, with isolated scenic elements); two- or three-fold sets (including conjoined composites).

Open-ended staging. The normal two-fold or three-fold (box set) formation of settings.

Enclosed settings. Four-walled settings; totally ceilinged sets. (Normally, both are best avoided if possible.)

Two-storey (*two-tiered*) *staging.* Normally one builds only at studio floor level to circumvent staging and production complications.

Area staging
Allows broad action and wide movement with emphasis on decorative or dramatic effect and pattern.

Table set-up
For localised action with emphasis on portraiture.

Audience show
May be a show in which an unseen studio audience watches normal studio action.

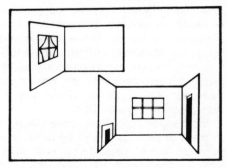

Open-ended staging
Two-fold set, or three-fold (box) set.

Types of Staging

TV staging is for the most part quite ephemeral. One could instance studios where the same setting, refurbished, has been left standing and used over again for many months' regular transmissions. But this form of *permanent setting* occupies costly studio floor-space and is not widely found. Even newscast and interview studios seek a frequent 'facelift'.

Standing sets

The 'permanent' or *standing sets* normally encountered in TV studios are those used for regularly recurring productions. Thus, a weekly quiz show will usually have the same familiar *stock set* for each appearance. Each episode of a soap opera, or a drama serial, will contain a stock set or two (e.g. the family's apartment), supplemented by a number of 'once only' settings built to suit the action of that particular episode. The 'permanent' sets may have been designed to form a *composite set* containing several adjacent rooms, halls, etc.—only those portions required for the specific episode being erected in the studio. Sets intended for re-use are sometimes reinforced to withstand the effects of continual handling and transportation. Otherwise they resemble routine standard settings.

Short-run staging

Most staging is for once-only construction, formed by juxtaposing a series of standard scenic units. For a single show, erected in the studio for a few hours at most, they provide a background for action (transmitted 'live' or video-taped), and are then dismantled (*struck*). Later these parts are segregated and stored with other similar *stock units*. Certain sections may have been hired from scenic suppliers, as will much of the furniture and the 'properties'. Other scenic parts may be salvaged for their materials, or junked rather than allowed to occupy valuable storage space.

Smaller studios using scenery for a single brief occasion may build from quite flimsy staging materials (page 62). But in the long term, re-usable units have much to recommend them. Effective staging may be achieved, however, with a minimum of scenic units, relying instead on the pictorial impact of light and shadow (pages 116-122, 140).

Scenic design can create its illusions, too, with large photographic or artist-painted backgrounds positioned behind performers. These may hang as vertical 'drops' ('backdrop', scenic cloth) (page 108), or be rear-projected (page 152).

Most ingenious of all, is the electronic wizardry that enables a subject in front of one camera to be inserted into the background from another picture-source (page 154). With such facilities as these, the sky's the limit for the scenic designer's opportunities.

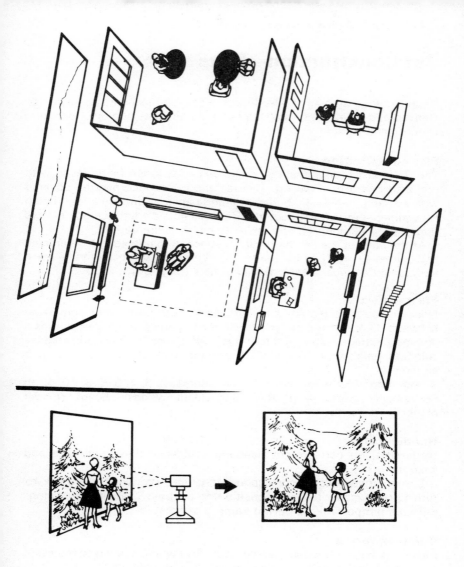

TYPES OF STAGING

Large composite setting

A series of adjacent interconnected sets together form a composite setting.
Typical examples include : office complexes, domestic interiors and interior/
exterior sets. The positions of all overhead bracing and suspension of scenery
must be agreed with the lighting director.

Backgrounds

Instead of built settings, backgrounds may be provided by flat vertical scenic
planes. Because the picture from the camera is two-dimensional (flat) it cannot
detect the falsity, unless background and foreground are unmatched.

21

Set Construction—Flats

Regular studio staging is based upon a series of standard scenic units. Derived and developed from stage and film practice, the most common of these is the studio *flat*.

Flat construction

The *flat* consists of a shallow, cross-braced wooden frame faced with prepared board or plywood. This rectangular surface may be covered with a stretched hessian, burlap or lining paper, to provide a foundation for wallpaper or textural treatment (canvas flats are lightweight, but are flimsy and lack rigidity). The entire assembly is fireproofed.

At the back of the flat, hardware is attached to enable it to be erected and joined to other units (page 24) 'Line and cleat' methods are a traditional *theatrical* means of joining flats (page 36).

Flattage sizes

Flats are constructed in 'standard sizes', but these vary somewhat between different studios, or television companies. In smaller studios a common flattage height of 8 to 9 ft is widely used. In 'network' studios, standard heights of 10 and 12 ft are more usual, with 9 and 14 ft extremes.

'Standard' widths for scenic flats include 1, 2, 3, 4, 5, 6, 8, 10, 12 ft. For smaller widths—e.g. 6 in, 9 in—plain wooden board (timber planking) is used.

Handling flats

Larger flattage can present handling problems, due to its size and weight.

Larger units become correspondingly more awkward, therefore, to move ('run') easily for exact positioning or rapid 'striking' (removing; perhaps temporarily, to permit camera access).

Complex forms

Most flats are single sided ('single clad'). But where a unit is to represent a wall with inside and outside surfaces, it is 'double clad'.

Curved flats are used less, but form the basis of decorative and contoured arrangements, and as small cycloramas.

The surface of flattage lends itself to a wide range of treatments, that can considerably alter its appearance (page 48).

Flat footage and metric equivalents

ft.	1	2	3	4	6	9	10	12
cm.	30·5	61	91	122	183	274	304	366

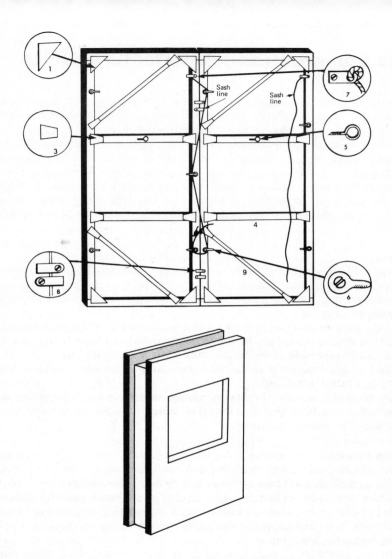

REGULAR SET CONSTRUCTION – FLATS

Scenic flat

The scenic flat is a single-sided plane surface of fireproofed hessian, $\frac{1}{4}$in. plywood, or prepared boarding, on a wooden frame.

The integral parts of the flat are:

1, Corner block; 2, Rail; 3, Keystone; 4, Toggle rail; 5, Brace eye;
6, Brace cleat; 7, Lash eye; 8, Stop cleats (to align flat on stile).
9, Diagonal brace.

Double-clad flat

Two single-sided flats fixed back to back are spaced (typically 6 ins. – standard brick size) to represent wall thickness.

23

Solid constructions that deceive the eye—but fit a scene truck.

Set Construction—Architectural Units

Where the setting includes decorative or architectural features such as doors, windows, fireplaces or niches, these are generally incorporated either as complete units, or introduced into contoured flats (frames).

Where a *complete* architectural unit is built, it comprises both the feature (e.g. a fireplace surround) and the flat it is fitted into. However, there are practical disadvantages to this construction. The height of the flat may be insufficient for a particular production (and may therefore need *topping up* to extend its height), or too high (and need *cutting down* to an appropriate height). The flat might also be of the wrong width.

Plugs

A more flexible scheme uses a *contoured flat* (frame) constructed with a cut-out area to take the corresponding *plug*. A particular plug can then be fitted into any of a number of standard graded flats with identical contoured openings.

Plugs may be built as hollow wooden structures, or as glass fibre or plastic shells, that bolt on to the contoured flat. Surface finish can be arranged to resemble wood, brick, stone, masonry, tiles, etc.

Door plugs include a range of styles, and encompass interior and exterior, glazed, solid, etc.

Occasionally, dummy fireplaces, doors, windows (or facsimiles) are attached to the face of a standard flat; when they are essentially non-practical (i.e. cannot be used).

Solid pieces

Solid pieces (rigid units, built pieces) are used to provide many free-standing architectural forms. They include such features as:

Pillars (columns, cylinders), 6 in to 2 ft in diameter, with heights of 2, 4, 8, 10 to 15 ft. (They are constructed of plywood on a timber frame, or of glass fibre. The latter is more easily carried, being lightweight, but is often less solid and stable.

Arches and half-arches. Usually of timber construction, these may need top-support for stability.

Stairs, staircases (straight and curved). They may be formed from *step units,* or a run of *treads* supported by a timber framework, surface-clad if necessary. Larger assemblies may require a steel scaffolding foundation structure.

Auxiliary architectural units are legion. These include the street furniture and ancillaries that dress the setting and consist of an inexhaustible list of lamp-posts, road signs, bus stops, mail boxes, fire hydrants, statuary, fencing, fountains, bollards, and so on. When one recalls the enormous variety of designs that are encountered for each of these common features, the set designer's problem here is evident.

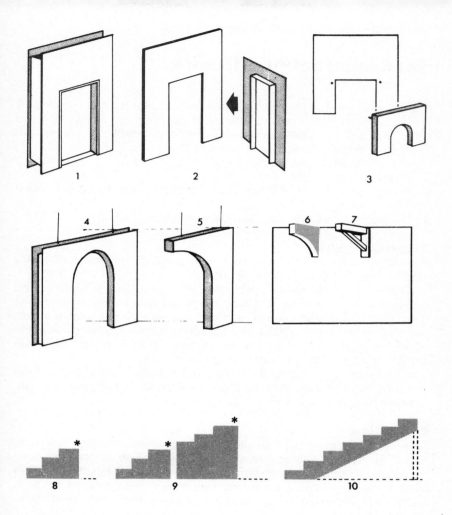

REGULAR SET CONSTRUCTION – ARCHITECTURAL UNITS

Architectural units
1, These may be permanently constructed, or fit into standard contoured flats or frames, as inserted 2 or screw-on plugs or shells 3.

Arches
Arches may be introduced as : 4, Complete arches (single or double clad) ;
5, Half arches (giving better camera access) ; 6, as a corbel (brace) to suggest a beam or arch ; 7, as an arched brace implying vaulting.

Stairways
They can be : 8, A three-step unit (3-tread stair unit) ; 9, Added to a higher unit to reach the next standard rostrum height ; 10, Run of treads to form a staircase. They may be legged up, or attached to rostra (e.g. by pin hinges), handrails fixed similarly.

25

The multi-purpose staging facility to create raised areas.

Set Construction—Rostra

Platforms of various standard heights are constructed from folding or interlocked frames (for easy transport and storage) with clip-on boarded tops. Their sides can be boarded-in (*clad*) and suitably decorated with hardboard, prepared board, contoured flats, etc.

Rostra form platforms for many purposes:
1. To provide raised flooring.
2. Architectural or natural floor-level variations (e.g. hillocks, uneven ground—page 52).
3. For multi-tier seating (e.g. audience, musicians, etc.).

Associated units

Stair units with 6 in risers (step heights) match the standard rostra heights (e.g. 1 ft 6 in, 2 ft, 4 ft, 6 ft).

Wooden *getaway steps* (*offstage steps*) provide performers with access points to rostra, so that they may avoid being seen on camera as they climb into position or exit, and also not become stranded at a high point. Sometimes visible stairs are inappropriate or unsuitable, particularly when the platform is to appear on camera, as an isolated unit. Then hidden getaway steps are used for access.

Ramps providing sloping flat surfaces from studio floor to rostrum top may be derived from standard flats, but are normally built from reinforced, non-slip boarding, and timber bracing.

Precautions

Care must be taken with all performer movement, seating, furniture, etc., on rostra, to guard against accidents. Wooden strips can limit side-slippage at rostrum edges, but for heights over about 2 ft, safety rails are often obligatory. Serious accidents have arisen through falls from high rostra, and anticipatory precautions are usually written into studio safety regulations.

Where extensive rostra are to be used, particularly when carrying heavy loads of people and/or equipment, such features are best built on a framework of specially erected steel scaffolding. Scaffold-board flooring is then clad in hardboard and suitably covered.

Blocks

Small raised areas may be produced by placing a series of block units side by side. These units are variously called blocks, risers, step-blocks, apple boxes. They are hollow wooden shells and come in many handy sizes from around 6 in×1 ft×1 ft, to a 2 ft cube. They have almost limitless applications, which include raising the height of furniture or actors for specific shots and to providing half-steps, decorative blocks, ground-height variations, plinths, etc.

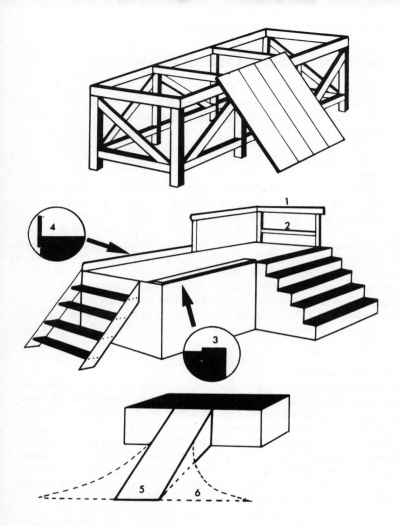

REGULAR SET CONSTRUCTION – ROSTRA (PLATFORMS, PARALLELS)

Rostra (platforms, parallels)
Each rostrum is formed from a permanent or folding frame. A detachable planking rostrum-top provides its floor. It is later surfaced with sound-proofing and facing-board. Sides can be boarded in (with plywood, hardboard, etc.) and decorated.

Safety measures
1, Handrails aid movement safety on the rostra ; 2, the kicking rail prevents people from slipping underneath the rail ; 3, wooden surface-strips or planks and 4, edge-strips prevent chairs, etc., from being pushed over the edge of the rostrum.

Ramps
5, Straight or 6, curved ramps fit standard rostra heights.

27

Set Construction—The Cyclorama

The cyclorama ('cyc' . . . pronounced 'sike') is a shallow, U-shaped construction, with a height of 9-15 ft, and typically some 20 to 60 ft long, or more.

Forms of cyclorama
The cyclorama can take various forms:

Solid cyc. This is a permanent installation, faced with a plywood or prepared board surface and may be provided in smaller studios, where the scene setting area is continually used. A smooth, even-toned and highly adaptable surface, it has the disadvantage, however, that it can focus and reflect sound to produce a hard audio quality or even 'slap back' (an echo effect).

Cyc cloth. Formed from canvas, duck or velours, the cloth can be hung and stretched from battens or tubular pipes, the bottom edge being floor-weighted to reduce creases. Some studios have a permanent cyc-track installed round their walls or the edge of the staging area. Stored *cyc-cloths* can then be clipped to the *cyc-rails'* runners and arranged to suit any staging layout.

The cyc's versatility
Cycs are among the most useful staging facilities, and are extensively used in television studios. They present a continuous unbroken surface that can form versatile backgrounds of many kinds, including neutral backgrounds (page 110), skies and decorated areas.

The cyclorama can be lit in a variety of ways, and may have patterns or shadows projected onto its surface (pages 114-118). One can attach scenic or decorative motifs to it, or use it to display painted or photographic backgrounds of all kinds. The regular cyc tones include off-white, light grey, dark grey, black, light blue and dark blue.

Hiding the bottom edge
Where the cyc and the floor are of similar tones, it becomes possible to blend them together to give an illusion of infinite space. Curved *cove* units (e.g. each 6 to 12 ft long) can be positioned at the bottom of the cyclorama to disguise the floor join. Plywood and glass-fibre forms are used. Alternatively, a ground row (page 30) may be used to provide successive scenic planes. Ground lighting units (cyc units) can be hidden behind the coves or ground rows to illuminate the lower parts of the cyclorama.

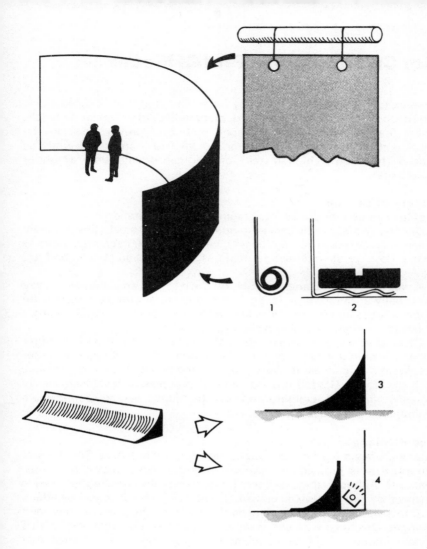

REGULAR SET CONSTRUCTION – THE CYCLORAMA

The cyclorama

The cyc-cloth is hung (edge-cleating) from a bar, barrel, or tubular cyc-rail. The lower edge is weighted to hold the cyc-cloth taut and wrinkle-free, by 1, wrapping it round a tubular bar or, 2, by means of numerous stage-weights.

The cove

This concave or sloping ramp unit helps to blend the floor with the cyc. It can be used 3, up against the cyc or, 4, a few feet from it, when ground lighting fittings can be hidden behind it, to illuminate the lower cyc surface.

Deceptively simple, but effective and economic.

Set Construction—Profile Pieces

Profiles (set pieces, cut-outs) may be constructed from sheets of ply-wood, compressed card, hardboard, prepared board or similar materials. These are invariably given a shaped outline or profile, and may be supported by a timber structure, or attached to a stock flat which is braced (hook-on or hinged jack), or weighted down (stage weight or sand bags).

Forms of profile
Profiles can be introduced into staging in various forms:

Decorative pieces may be free standing or slung by steel cable as purely ornamental devices (fretting, tracery, wrought work, decorative panels) (page 126), or as architectural features (columns, archways, bridges, etc.).

Wings are vertical planes masking off the edges of an acting area. They are usually in the form of 'foliage', or architectural profiles, and may be surface-contoured for a more realistic effect (e.g. brick or rock surfacing), or based on a photographic blow-up.

Ground rows are simple vertical planes (perhaps with profiled edges), standing a few feet from the bottom of a cyclorama or other scenic unit, to conceal its *floor-join* (i.e. the line its lower edge makes with the floor). Graded ground rows of progressive height are occasionally introduced. Lighting units can be hidden behind ground rows to illuminate subsequent planes.

Scenic planes
Scenic planes are a frequent application for profile pieces. This type of ground row is profiled to represent hills, rooftops, distant buildings, trees, etc. Although they are flat in form, in carefully arranged successive planes they can achieve a surprisingly realistic three-dimensional effect, due to parallactic movement between them as the camera viewpoint changes. Designed with exaggerated perspective, and enhanced with a certain amount of surface modelling (e.g. stuck-on detail) an illusion of distance may be built up quite cheaply, as a substitute for more elaborate scenic arrangements. One should always aim at a maximum distance between such ground rows, in order to provide optimum lighting treatment. Below a 6 ft minimum, there may be insufficient room for lamp units, or to permit light spread.

REGULAR SET CONSTRUCTION – PROFILE PIECES

Decorative pieces
The stylised units here show a pillar, arch, and even the gondola, all in flat construction, yet effective in a theatrical application.

Wings
From the front, this profile-piece appears naturalistic at more distant viewpoints. The reverse shows its construction and the stage brace holding the assembly up.

Scenic Planes (ground rows)
Here a series representing mountain ranges hides lamps in a ground-trough.

31

Drapes

Drapes (draperies) is the generic term for all fabrics used in staging—whether hung as scenic backgrounds, or as set-dressings providing window curtains, tapestries, decorative cloths, etc.

Occasionally the entire staging may be derived from drapes, but where applied *en masse*, they are more usually arranged as a foil to free-standing or slung scenic elements (e.g. panels, screens, pillars). So we find pleated grey velour drapes, for example, used as a general-purpose background for programmes as diverse as discussions and dance routines.

Methods of support

Drapes can be supported by several standard methods:

Slung from a suspended batten or tubular metal bar.

Hung from overhead rail or pulley systems (tab-rail, tab-track, traveler), or from a fixture attached to the staging (wall-batten, runner, trackway).

Hung over flats, the surplus being secured at the rear.

Hung on a drape frame: this is a single, two- or three-fold lightweight timber or tubular-metal framework.

Hung on a gallows arm, which may be affixed directly or by pin-hinging to scenery, to provide rapid access and avoid floor obstruction.

Directly attached to flats by tacking, stapling, or curtain hooks on a string.

Words of warning

The following general observations on the use of drapes in staging should be noted:

● Storage folds, creasing, stains, dirtying, can appear prominent, even over-emphasised on camera.

● Try to avoid materials with small patterns (which can appear fussy), thin vertical or horizontal stripes, or close checks (they cause strobing) or distinctive recognisable patterns (they limit reuse).

● Very dark toned or light-absorbent materials (velvets, velours) tend to look drab, and nearby surfaces may become over-bright in the strong lighting needed to model them.

● Very light toned materials must usually be 'taken down' (darkened) by dipping, spraying, or black gauze covering.

● Shadows of structural framework when seen through rear-illuminated drapes are distorted by the draping.

● Drapes with a glazed or glossy finish may provide enhanced modelling, or embarrassing hotspots, according to luck.

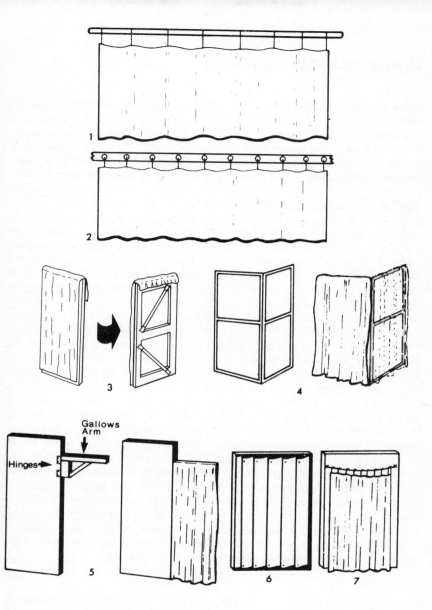

DRAPES

Hanging systems

These include : 1, Suspended bar ; 2, Tab-rail (traveler) ; 3, Hung over a flat ;
4, Drape frame ; 5, Gallows arm ; 6, Pleated and tacked (or stapled) to a flat ;
7, Hooked on to string fastened across a flat.

Plans and Elevations

Although staging, like production treatment, can be carried out on a 'try-it-and-see' basis, the process is far too inefficient and time consuming for regular TV practice. Instead, all operations, from the 'gleam in the directors' eye' stage to the complete video recording or live transmission, are systematically planned and scheduled long before the show hits the studio floor. To the designer, the plan is all important.

The plan and its derivatives

Much of this planning is carried out on scale drawings of the studio staging area (typical scales $\frac{1}{4}$ in = 1 ft, 1: 50, etc.). On this *studio plan,* the positions of various features are printed (entrances, stairways, supply points for electricity, water or steam, storage areas, and adjacent service areas such as make-up, quick change rooms, fire lanes, etc.). Supplies for technical facilities are indicated, such as camera plugging panels, lighting hoists, lighting and camera crane power. Scenic hoists, catwalks, grids, access and stacking areas, cyc-rails, are all of direct interest to the designer and director when arranging staging for a show.

Upon the squared staging (setting) area, outlines are drawn for the production, showing the sets and major scenic features (e.g. floor painting, trees, etc.). When the staging is erected in the studio, this plan will exactly determine the position of all units.

Subsequently, the director works out his action treatment. To this *staging plan* (*setting plan*) is added a detailed *furniture plot,* showing the positions of all furniture items. Assistants may, on larger scale plans, prepare even more detailed *prop.* (*property*) *plots*, showing where strategic props., working apparatus, etc., is to be located.

The director, having planned his production treatment, then draws upon the TV staging plan, the positions, moves (and, perhaps, cabling) of his studio cameras. This is examined by various technical specialists (relative to staging operations, technical directions, lighting, sound, etc.) who assess potential hazards and co-ordinate their work effort.

The lighting director, for example, will use this information to devise a lighting plot, indicating the total treatment for the production.

Elevations

We see, therefore, that the staging plan is of considerable importance to all concerned with the planning and organisation of the production. A parallel document used for all staging interpretation and construction is the *elevation*. This gives dimensional details of 'side views' of all scenery, showing building and erection features, architectural items, surface finish, etc. A large studio production may require several sheets of elevations to encompass all the settings and their constructional data, but only one staging plan (with its progressive embellishments) will be used throughout. Copies are sent to the respective specialists.

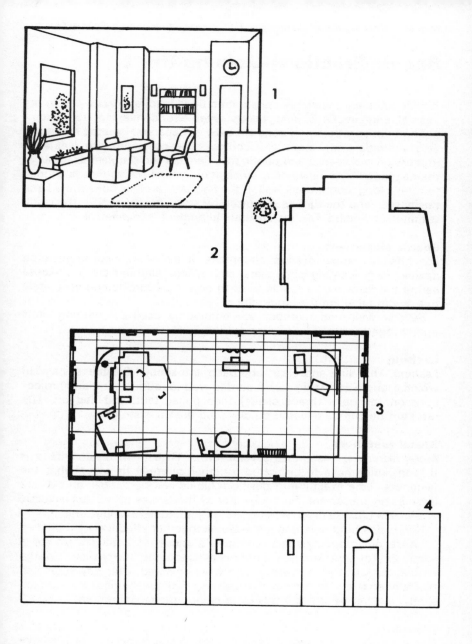

PLANS AND ELEVATIONS

Drawings

1, Sketch ; 2, Setting plan ; 3, Studio staging plan ; 4, Elevations.

35

With careful setting the separate scenic units merge into a total environment.

Scenic Erection—Joining Units

Scenic units are invariably constructed as individual pieces—or, in the case of large erections, in segments suitable for convenient handling.

Although some staging units are used as separate, isolated structures (e.g. a single tree), many will conjoin with other units to create an impression of expanse and continuity. Perhaps the simplest example of the combined effect is when a series of individual scenic flats is aligned to form a long, continuous wall. If the flats are carefully constructed and positioned, and their joints disguised by stripping (page 52), the result is quite convincing. Clearly, accurate alignment is imperative.

Scenic alignment
For effective edge-to-edge alignment, units often require location devices (e.g. locating pins, metal stop cleats, aligning blocks). These permit the faces of the scenic units to be set up quickly and accurately to a 'setting line' on the studio floor.

Several well-tried methods are commonly used for holding units tightly together.

Lashing
Lashing. This 'line and cleat' approach is a simple, flexible system, in which a length of attached sash cord is wound round alternating projections on the units (brace cleats) then pulled taut, and tied off. The resultant tie can be released quickly, and the units struck.

Metal fasteners
Metal fasteners. These take several forms. Their main disadvantage is that the units have to be mated together carefully to ensure that the fasteners come exactly into position. Limits can be critical, and where large heavy pieces are involved, other methods may prove less irksome.

L-plates provide drop-in fasteners for joining lightweight units.

Wing-nuts hold indented edge-plates together effectively.

Loose *pin-hinge* connections have a range of applications, for a single pin (or bent wire nail) not only clips together the two parts of the fixture, but provides a swing-hinge where needed. Getaway steps can be fastened (top and bottom, if necessary) with pin-hinges for maximum safety, and yet be struck easily by removing their locating pins.

Clamps
Quick-fix clamps (cramps). These clamps, of adjustable jaw-width, have the merit of being adaptable to structures of various shapes and sizes, and in holding units together extremely firmly. On the other hand, they are detachable (and costly) fittings that are comparatively heavy, and liable to be mislaid.

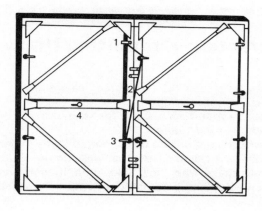

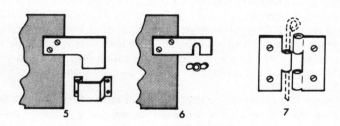

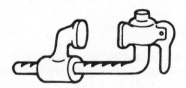

SCENIC ERECTION AND SUPPORT

Lashing

Sashcord lashes adjacent flats together firmly. 1, Lash-eye, a drilled plate or screw-eye through which a sashline is knotted ; 2, Sashline ; 3, Brace cleat provides an anchoring stub ; 4, Brace-eye for stage brace.

Metal fasteners

Fixed at the edge of scenic units, enabling them to be clipped together.
5, L-plate fitting ; 6, U-plate and wing nut ; 7, Pin-hinge with removable pin to release fitting.

Adjustable clamp (cramp)

Holds units of various thicknesses tightly together.

Rapid setting and striking of staging requires simple, flexible methods of scenic support.

Scenic Erection Supporting Units

Scenic units may be placed into three broad categories:
1. Units that are *self-supporting*.
2. Units that need *support aid*, usually for safety.
3. Units that require *total support*.

   Staging often needs not only to be supported firmly in position, but to be held rigid, too. We have to ensure that walls do not shudder as doors close, or handrails shake when held, and so on. If, moreover, a door flat is not correctly erected and held, the door within it may stick or prove troublesome to use.

The stage brace
Special devices have been introduced for scenic support. The commonest is undoubtedly the *stage brace*. This is an extending wooden prop of adjustable length.

   At its top end, is a C- or U-shaped fitting that hooks into a metal loop, or plate on the scenery. A screw-eye at the rear of flats is normally used for this purpose. Alternatively, the top of the brace may be fitted with a rod at right angles to the stem, that can be slipped into holed plates in the studio wall (wall-eyes).

   At the lower end of the stage brace a metal strut of flat strip is fitted. This enables the brace to be weighed down by a heavy cast-iron *stage-weight* or a small sandbag. Struts are sometimes drilled so that a *stage-screw* can be inserted, to fix the brace end extremely rigidly into installed floor sockets. But this rather unusual method means that staging positions must correspond to these screw joints distributed around the studio.

Fitted supports
Jacks (*hinged base, French brace*) are hinged triangular struts screwed to the rear of units. Unfolded at right angles, they are held down by stage weights or sandbags. For small pieces such as low profiles, ground rows and runs of low horizontal flats, jacks can provide quite compact, convenient methods of unit support.

   Lightweight free-standing planes are sometimes fitted with a 'weight shelf'. This takes the form of a horizontal plank at the foot, attached by metal angle shelf supports, and is held down firmly with stage weights or sandbags. Simple in concept, this idea is convenient as a method of supporting transparent, translucent, or mesh screens, cases where other systems would be conspicuous from the camera position.

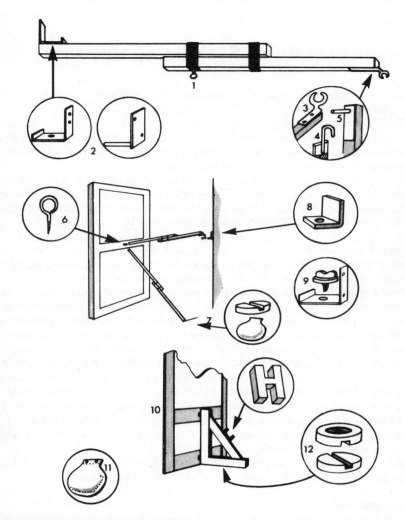

SCENIC ERECTION AND SUPPORT

Stage brace
After length adjustment, the extensible stage-brace is held firm with a thumb screw (1). At its lower end: 2, Brace iron or bar. At its upper end: 3, Claw-hook, or 4, C-hook, or 5, bar.

Supporting flats
6, At its top end the brace hooks into a brace-eye or plate on the flat; 7, The brace iron at its lower end is securely weighted by a sandbag or stage weight, or inserted into a wall plate 8. Occasionally a stage screw 9, is utilised.

Jack (French brace, hinged brace)
A hinged strut at the rear of a scenic unit, 10. May be weighted down with canvas sandbags, 11, or stage weights, 12, of different kinds (H-type or plate type).

39

Safety depends upon secure scenic erection.

Scenic Erection—Stabilising Scenery

Certain structures are inherently unstable, particularly if they are high, narrow-based, top-heavy, or relatively unsupported.

Stability requirements range from simply ensuring that the construction will not fall over, to permitting people to lean or walk on them. In the ultimate case they should withstand the use of shoulders or even battering rams to burst through locked doors.

Timber straps. The simplest method of ensuring stability is to nail or screw timber straps (e.g. 3 in×1 in section) across the rear of adjoining units, virtually making them into one. However, this is time consuming, both to introduce and dismantle. It can also lead to unit damage.

Regular methods
Bottom weighting. For a small, isolated unit (e.g. pillars, trees) stage-weights or sandbags can be used to weight it at the base.

Suspension lines. Steel cables or ropes can be dropped from the studio's ceiling grid, roof support girders, or similar load-bearing members to enable scenic units to be steadied or suspended in position. These are tied or clipped to *hanging-irons* (metal straps with loops and rings), affixed to the top rails of flats, and scenic units; as shown on the designer's elevations. Hoists have generally supplanted earlier block and tackle facilities. They provide safety suspension for heavy or unbalanced scenic pieces, including high walls, ceilings, roofs, trees and columns. They can be used, too, to hang lightweight scenic dressings and equipment (e.g. drapes, chandeliers, branches, shadow gobos).

In high studios, these suspension lines may be used to *fly* scenery up to the studio roof, to clear the studio floor.

For fine positioning or steadying we can *brail* an item over from its *dead* position (where it hangs naturally) by a *brail line* (scenic cord).

Problem cases
Bracing struts. These are lengths of timber (e.g. 3 in×1 in section) nailed to the tops of flats across the corner angles of walls, or between facing units. Bracing is applied after erection, where other methods of support are insufficient or impracticable. So, where stage braces cannot be hidden, or a door flat is unbalanced, or a wall only attached to the rest of a structure by one end, judiciously placed bracing struts may save the day. They should, of course, be introduced only in collaboration with lighting design, for such struts can cause distracting shadows.

Floor spiking. In the motion picture industry, units and their timber stays may be firmly nailed or screwed to the studio floor. Film dollies can move smoothly on their transportable rails, or 'tracks' across uneven floor. But spiking is forbidden in the TV studio, because an even level floor is a prerequisite of smooth, mobile camerawork.

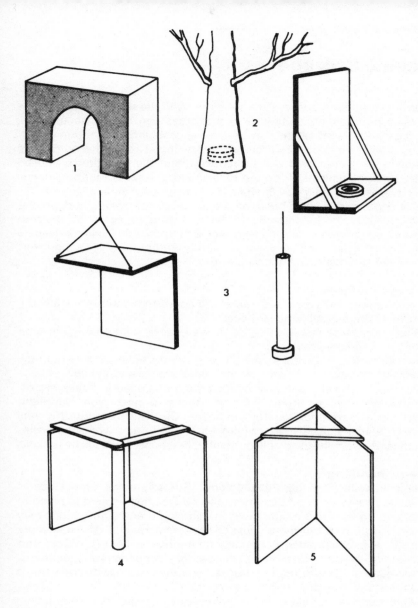

SCENIC ERECTION AND SUPPORT

Stabilising scenery

1, Scenic units may be sufficiently stable to be self-supporting ; 2 Sometimes bottom weighting will give top-heavy units sufficient stability; 3, Wire slings or ropes can provide top support, or stabilise units :— Attached to hanging-irons ; 4, Bracing struts to nearby units can anchor an isolated piece ; 5, Corner bracing by timber nailed across adjacent flats holds them rigid.

41

Scenic Storage

In most TV stations, space is at a premium. With the staging requirements of daily productions, settings and properties can rapidly accumulate. Storage and classification can become a problem. By continually re-using scenic units in a refurbished or revamped form, the number of actual stock pieces held can be reduced, and the quantity of unused *dead stock* minimised. If, on the other hand, the same routine stock is over-worked day after day, staging design can be stultified.

The economic balance between the technique of making and junking new staging or, alternatively, of holding staging as stock units in expensive storage space until they may be required, is clearly a delicate one. Some items can be used frequently without being recognised; others are too distinctive for regular use.

Storage methods
Baskets (hampers) wire-cage trucks and containers, multi-tier shelving, help to accommodate smaller items.

Flattage may be stored in racks, or wall packs (laid one against the other) in standard sizes.

Scenic cloths, backdrops, sky-drops or photo enlargements, can be rolled and rack-stored. Drapes can be folded and basket-stored.

Furniture, suitably protected by covers, can be piled and rack-stored.

How far a station holds its own stocks or hires from suppliers, becomes a matter for careful judgment. Clearly, to continually hire certain regularly used items would be uneconomic, while the maintenance of a seldom-used collection of general bric-a-brac is unrealistic.

Scenic handling
Scenic handling too has its problems. Strongly-made timber scenic units are heavy. Their robustness has to be weighed against the labour, time, and transportation difficulties in handling them. Lighter units may be easier to move, but more liable to become damaged. Much scenery these days is constructed from glass-fibre which is light in weight and resistant to damage. Flats, fireplaces, masonry, statuary, pillars, columns, balustrades, walls, paving, tree trunks, windows, archways, shop fronts and roofs will be made from this material.

Motorised scenic trucks, pallet conveyance, tug and trailer equipment can all ease scene transport problems. Within the studio, electric hoists and handling aids can facilitate scene erection by speeding operations and reducing the manpower needed.

Accidental damage by crushing, tearing, breakage or just dirtying in transit are constant hazards. A torn or dirty wallpapered flat can be repaired after erection. Other items, some possibly hired, might not. So care and methodical organisation are essential.

SCENIC STORAGE
Props cage
A metal-framed mobile unit, fitted with welded-mesh sides for security in transporting props.

Props store
Multi-tier shelving units (furniture sheeted over) and storage basket.

Scenic storage methods
1, Wall pack ; 2, Suspended scenery ; 3, Scenic rack ; 4, Scenic truck for transportation, pulled by electric tug ; 5, Box-contained cyc-cloth (hamper) ; 6, Wall rack for rolled scenic cloths, etc.

43

Scenic Tone and Finish

If scenic tones exceed the camera's contrast range, they will be lost.

If a surface is too bright for the camera tube, it reproduces as plain, white and unmodelled (*block-off, crush or bloom*). We lose all surface detail (e.g. printed pages look blank!), lose contouring (light-toned objects appear as flat white areas), and colour becomes 'bleached out' (shiny highlights reproduce as white blobs). Glossy areas can cause distracting highlights, reflect onto faces, emphasise picture defects (*streaking, lag*).

Over-bright areas

Over-bright areas result from too light a surface, excessive illumination, over-exposure (camera lens aperture too large), wrong electronic adjustment (e.g. too little tube beam-current), or bounced light reflections towards a particular camera angle.

Blowing down an over-light region (airbrush, aerosol spray, or brushing with black or grey paint) can produce a greying or *dirtied down* result if overdone.

Shiny surfaces may be wax-sprayed, water-pasted, or putty daubed to dull them, or might have to be re-angled or removed altogether. Too many dull, matte surfaces around and the overall effect lacks sparkle, looks dead and uninteresting. Too much glass, chromium, silver, and light reflections predominate.

Over-dark areas

Areas that are too dark, reproduce as murky, undetailed, poorly modelled regions marred by the random, scintillating specks of video noise. This happens where materials are themselves too dark-toned, have excessive light absorption (as with deep velvet), or when insufficient light falls upon them (light is often cut off by shadowing or shading), through under-exposure or, electronic adjustment (low 'black level').

Tonal limits

Most TV studios staging aims to restrict scenic tones to certain prescribed limits. This *grey scale* indicates in measured steps, progressive reflectance values from a minimum of $3\frac{1}{2}$% to a maximum of 70%. Scenic paints are classified according to their equivalent Munsell grey values.

Ideally, all scenic tones, furnishing, set dressings, properties, should observe these tonal restrictions and lighting should not unduly increase these contrast values. In practice, such theoretical limits serve rather as guiding restraints, and corrective measures are taken wherever the pictorial effect is unsatisfactory. Sometimes light levels can be adjusted on extreme scenic tones; sometimes the offending surface itself has to be altered—e.g. a darker table-covering used, glass removed from a wall picture, a hot-spot covered up.

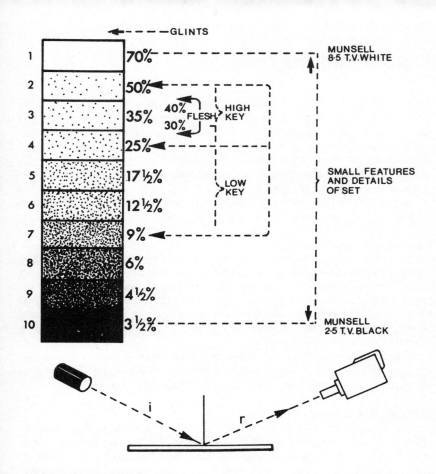

SCENIC TONES AND FINISH

The grey scale

In this tonal wedge, each step is $\sqrt{2}$ times the brightness of the next, their relative light reflectances in percentages being shown on the right. The logarithmic scale looks linear to the eye, so that an apparent mid-grey reflects only $17\frac{1}{2}\%$ of incident light, not the 50% one might expect.

Studio paints and materials are compared on camera with the standard grey scale, and classified accordingly, to identify and interrelate tonal values. Accepted maximum scenic and subject contrasts should not generally exceed around 2:1 for large adjacent areas, 5:1 for large non-adjacent areas and 20:1 for small adjacent areas. Final tonal values will depend upon incident light level and contrast, shadowing, exposure, video adjustment, surface angles, texture and perception effects.

Light reflection

When the incident angle of the light (i) and the angle of the camera to the surface coincide (i.e. with the reflected angle of the light, r) light reflections from that surface are at their maximum. They may prove excessive, even from dark surfaces.

Put a frame round part of any scene, and the forms and colour within it immediately develop new relationships.

Colour and the Designer

The world around us is in colour, and even when a designer is creating exclusively for a 'black and white' TV system, he will invariably express himself in terms of naturalistic hues. But, however pleasing the effect of colour may be before the camera, the designer for a monochrome medium must always reconcile himself to the fact that an effective image is dependent upon a good translation into grey scale tones. The attraction or significance of colour in the studio has no value to his audience. Indeed, distinctly different hues can become identical shades of grey in the monochrome picture!

Compatible colour
Colour TV complicates the situation further. The colour relationships, decorative effects, coloured lighting treatment, that are part of staging appeal for the colour TV audience, are still lost to viewers watching on monochrome receivers. Worse still, we find that the audience impact of effective colour staging may translate differently in terms of light and shade. Thus, a 'blue summer sky' can in monochrome become a 'thunderous, threatening grey sky'!

In designing for colour TV, whether for settings, costume, make-up, lighting, graphics, one must consider both compatible monochrome and translated colour, and aim to satisfy both forms of the medium.

Staging for colour
Colour has an attraction; too much if not controlled. Colour has its associations—sometimes inappropriate ones. Colour is dynamic. This is an embarrassment when we are seeking delicate, subtle, subdued, or sordid effects. Colour too easily become brash, vulgar, cheap, tawdry, exaggerated, tiring to watch.

Further, the hue before the camera may not be reproduced accurately in the coloured picture. A rich purple may be modified to a violet hue. A blue or green surface can become more vivid.

Generally speaking, staging for colour makes extensive use of paled pastel colours, of greyed and darkened hues. Colour emphasis is achieved through the use of colour in costume, set dressings and properties, rather than through large scenic areas of colour. Colour easily dominates a scene even when defocused. Specular reflections in in coloured surfaces usually appear as white blobs of light. Certain colour mixtures can reveal dissimilarities between intercut cameras, so that they become, for example, a reddish brown in one shot, but a greenish fawn on another. One area of colour can modify the apparent hue of a subject positioned in front of it. Thus, caucasian skin can look pale, red, tanned, yellowish, according to its background hue. (It tends towards the complementary colour of its surroundings.)

The viewer and monochrome

However effective colour may be in the studio or on a colour system, the viewer watching a black and white picture is only influenced by the grey-scale values.

Colour attraction

Colour can attract, but it can distract too.

Colour domination

1, Strong background hues are overpowering, and influence flesh-tone reproduction ; 2, Colour is more readily controlled if strong hues are present only in costume, set dressings and properties.

47

Surface Treatment

A remarkable variety of surface treatments can be achieved just by the way in which one applies the standard casein paints, distempers, and water-based media. In addition to the even-toned, textureless surface painting of a *flat lay-in*, one can, by over-spraying, create shading effects, pseudo contouring, dirtying, and similar unevenness. This matte finish may be further altered by a second coating, which blends another colour or tone. A light varnish gloss can provide a controlled sheen or, more generously applied, suggest a wet surface.

Textural effects

Dry-brush work overpaints a dry flat ground colour with a nearly dry brush, the brushmark pattern looking like wood, metal, stone or fabric.

Stippling with small close dots or patterns (by coarse brush, sponge, screwed paper, cloth) suggests earth, cement or stone.

Puddling interflows colours for ageing plaster, walls, etc.

Daubing with a rolled rag (paper, or sponge too) changes tone density.

Scumbling of a dark tone over light, or *glazing* with dry-brushed light tones over dark, creates shading or highlight texture.

Gentle *dragging* (*scuffing*) of paint lightly skims the surface and emphasises its irregularities.

A *wash* of lighter or darker tone over a background (body) colour simulates highlights and shadows.

Dottling (*spattering*) mottles with random brush-thrown splashes. Also successfully achieved by using a spray-gun at low pressure.

Rough-cast by sprinkling sawdust or powder irregularly on the wet paint introduces textural and tonal variations.

Scenic artists can paint flats to appear as brick, stonework, panelling, fabric, grained wood, etc. But such counterfeiting requires time and experience. Instead, wallpaper or plastic roll-sheeting facsimiles, or photo reproductions can be used, augmented perhaps with artist-painted surface details or surface work.

General decorative surface treatment for staging may use, in addition to the above techniques, commercial wallpapers, roller-printing, stencilled motifs, attached panels, stuck-on motifs (paper, plastic sheet, photographic); fabric surfacing, as well as artist-painted work.

Attached contouring

Unfortunately, oblique or close viewpoints or cast shadows soon reveal the falsity of imitation contouring on a flat surface. Then it may become necessary to use actual three-dimensional modelling formed from plastic, papier mâché, carved wood, glass-fibre or rubber mouldings, or plastic vacuum-formed shell contours. All these can provide convincing brickwork, stonework, woodwork, surface moulding, carving, tiling, cornices, panelling, tree bark, etc., of many kinds.

SURFACE TREATMENT

Surface treatment
The method of application influences the appearance of the finished result.
There are many techniques : 1, Sprayed ; 2, Brushed ; 3, Dragged, scuffing,
dry-brushed ; 4, Puddling ; 5, Daubing with paper, rag, or sponge ; 6, Dottling,
spattering.

Stencilled outlines
Stencilled outlines blown by a spray gun, using foliage, expanded metal mesh,
fishnet, etc.

Shell contours
Glass fibre and vacuum-moulded plastic provide deep contouring and
lightweight construction. They are readily cut up, conjoined and stapled to
timber and standard flats.

TVS-D

After-Treatment of Staging

After-treatment of staging in the studio tends to be of three kinds—improvement, corrective and atmospheric.

Improvement
Immediately after its construction, the studio staging has a fresh, clean, pristine look. But if staging is left in this raw state, its appearance on camera may be rather disappointing. Most settings benefit from judicious after-treatment. Carefully applied shading (by airbrush, spray, light brushing) can bring out surface modelling and the shape of structures. Plain flat surfaces can be given a subtle texturing that overcomes an otherwise blank, uninteresting finish. Skilful lighting can substitute or augment this after-treatment, but this can prove time-consuming.

Corrective
Initially, corrective treatment involves refurbishing any storage, handling, or transportation damage. Accidentally torn or dirtied wallpaper, scrapes or breakages, can occur, despite care.

Later, during camera rehearsals, corrections will be made to rectify any staging errors or misjudgments the camera reveals, e.g. removing embarrassing reflections, repainting unsuitable decor. There are always peripheral jobs such as ensuring that a cyc. cloth is free of wrinkles, that a lampshade is straight, improving the disposition of set dressing, and these form an important part of the creative set designer's activities during rehearsal.

Atmospheric
Expert atmospheric after-treatment can transform the simpler setting into a wholly convincing illusion. Perceptively shaded walls, slight shading or highlighting with sprayed pigments around light switches, door handles, rub marks on walls, create a lived-in feel that is elusive to define.

Known variously as *blowing down, antiquing, dirtying-down*, this localised spraying and discoloration at door frames, corners, crevices, fireplaces, picture edges, wall fittings, windows, etc., simulates grime and wear-marks, where such effects accumulate in actual locations.

Carried to extremes, or crudely over-emphasised, we have slummy, neglected or delapidated results. These have their place in the set designer's repertoire, together with dust (Fuller's earth) and cobwebs (specially blown fine rubber filaments), but one must guard against inadvertently creating ageing or dirtiness in more normal staging.

AFTER-TREATMENT OF STAGING

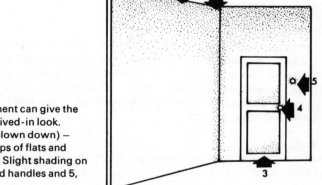

The fresh construction
Freshly decorated scenery can have a raw, artificial look.

Subtle treatment
Selective after-treatment can give the set a more authentic lived-in look. 1, Slightly sprayed (blown down) – darker towards the tops of flats and towards corners 2; 3, Slight shading on door panels, 4, around handles and 5, light switches.

Ageing treatment
Emphasised after-treatment introduces a dingy, slummy look; 6, Water staining; Uneven colour wash; 7, Heavier, uneven spraying; 8, Dark marks around handle and switch; 9, Scuff marks on door and wall; 10, Rub marks on wall and doorway; 11, Chair scrape on wall; 12, Lighter wall tone (cover up when spraying) shows 'removal' of picture from the wall!

51

Staging Devices—Disguising Joins

When scenic units are placed side by side, however tightly held together, there is invariably a crack between them that betrays their individual construction. In a run of plain flats, such joins are particularly noticeable. We may even see studio lights through them. There are several ways of disguising the edge joins.

Stripping
Simplest is *stripping* (*Dutchman, rhinoceros hide*), in which narrow paper or fabric strips are pasted along the joins. This treatment can only be applied in the studio, to the erected setting, and may be destroyed if adjacent flats are later re-angled. Wallpaper stripping usually requires carefully matched patterns.

Breaks
Staging sometimes avoids edge joins by introducing *breaks* in which a flat is displaced, being stood in front of or behind its neighbours. Although most effective in decorative staging, where the planar displacement can provide attractive effects, this technique can usually only be applied in architectural staging when the discontinuities are unseen by the camera.

Returns
Most familiar of all, is the *return (jog)*, in which the run of the wall is interrupted and a buttress or recess, for example, deliberately created by introducing a narrow flat typically 3 in, 6 in, 9 in, up to 2 ft wide, lap-joined at right angles. This results in more interesting, broken-up wall lines, and somewhat improved acoustics. By far the best design solution to the problem of disguising scenic joins, is by creating returns 'naturally' using architectural variations to break up planes. As a bonus, this avoids the use of precious studio time and labour, that stripping involves.

CONSTRUCTIONAL DEVICES –
DISGUISING JOINS

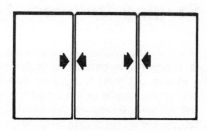

Stripping
The cracks between conjoining flats are concealed behind narrow paper or fabric strips stuck over them.

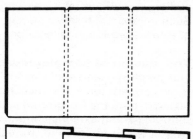

Breaks
Joins can sometimes be disguised by *breaks* which conceal the confines of individual scenic units.

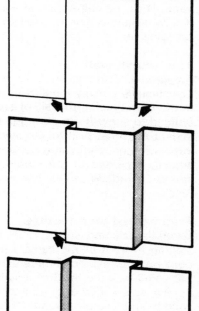

Returns (jogs)
A regular method of disguising joins between flats. Where return flats are not seen on camera, they may be omitted.

Staging Devices—Disguising Extent

Given half a chance, the camera picture can readily suggest that staging is much more extensive (or much more limited) than it really is. As viewers, we tend to assume that because we are looking at part of an environment, the rest is also there if only we could see it. In designing for the camera, therefore, we can take advantage of this false premise, and deliberately curtail the staging to show only just enough to satisfy the audience with visual clues suggesting completeness, and no more. Such an approach saves money, space, time, and forms the foundation of shrewd productional economies.

The illusion of completeness
The simplest example of this technique is when a foreground performer is positioned some distance from a background scene. The camera, taking in both the foreground and background, combines them, implying that the setting extends continuously, from the distance right up to the person in the foreground. In reality, only empty floor space may intervene. Thus, a small setting area may appear to be spacious, particularly if a wide-angle lens is used to shoot the scene, and so exaggerate perspective.

The 'fourth wall'
Foreground features such as furniture, doorways, arches, windows, can similarly convey the illusion of scenic extent. They can suggest the presence of the 'fourth wall' of a room, even although the camera is never obliged to show it. So strong is this illusion, that we can even shoot a distant plain flat past an isolated foreground subject, and still gain an impression of solidity and depth in the picture. Where the fourth wall is actually included in the studio set, continuous camera, lighting and sound operations usually become unduly complicated and limited as a result.

Fragmented architecture
Carefully selected scenic units can be arranged to suggest that the staging in front of the camera takes a particular form that in reality it does not. For example, three flats and a handrail can be interpreted by the camera as the head of a staircase; a few well-positioned flats can appear as a series of adjoining rooms. One is led to misconstrue the solidity and shape of architecture that does not exist!

In more sophisticated applications of this technique, the designer can build half an arch, a section of a pillar, part of a window, and yet leave the viewer with the firm conviction that he has seen the entire feature, particularly if the complete scene has already been shown (e.g. on a film insert or graphic) as matching with the studio replica.

54

CONSTRUCTIONAL DEVICES –
DISGUISING EXTENT

Foreground action
1, Location of foreground subjects can suggest that scenic continuity exists between the foreground and distant staging – although in reality, there is only *space* in between. Intervening set dressing aids the illusion.
2, Even where no staging is involved at all, the effect can still be quite convincing.

1

2

Foreground scenery
Scenic foreground pieces suggest architectural relationships, even when the visual clues are nominal.

Selective sections
Selective sections are interpreted on the screen as having solidity and continuity. If carefully positioned, they imply a complete structure.

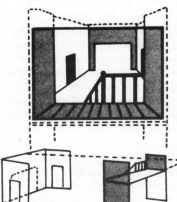

Staging Devices—Using Perspective

In everyday life, as objects move away from us, their effective size seems to diminish. The spaces between equidistant telegraph poles appear to lessen with distance, railway tracks look as if they are converging as they disappear towards the horizon. All this kind of common daily experience of *perspective* can be put to use in TV staging to emphasise or falsify the impression of space and size in the picture.

The illusion of space
Distance and depth in a scene can be conveyed by as simple a subterfuge as a painted flat scenic backing, or a photographic enlargement including perspective. Its lowest edge is merged with a painted studio floor, or suitably disguised, to give a continuous effect.

We can deliberately include a series of scenic planes between foreground and background to aid the illusion of depth and distance.

These planes can be arranged to contain false clues to enhance the spatial effect. So we might introduce larger tables, wall lamps, wall pictures in areas near the camera viewpoint, while using progressively smaller items further from the camera. This kind of deliberate size-arrangement can be quite subtle, and unlike more blatant faking, does not appear false when seen from camera angles other than the one for which it is primarily designed.

Scale distortion
Scenic distortion can produce intriguing, dramatic effects when introduced into staging. In *scale distortion*, an entire setting and its furnishings are built of larger or smaller size than normal, in order to make performers appear tiny or gigantic.

Falsifying perspective in staging
False perspective (forced perspective) deliberately provides changes in size and proportions of distant planes, to convey the impression of depth and extension to the studio setting. Although only strictly accurate for one pre-arranged camera position, in practice some variation in the viewpoint is usually possible. However, we must always ensure that no shadows from performers or scenery fall upon the surfaces of the false perspective planes and reveal their true form. The direction and contrast of lighting, too, should match throughout.

Occasionally, the distant part of a setting can be built in exaggerated perspective, rather in the form of a large-scale model.

In the extreme, the entire set may be constructed with the diminution of perspective. However, this technique has the drawback that scale errors arise if people move upstage, away from the camera. The camera viewpoint is essentially critical, and staging can become needlessly complex.

CONSTRUCTIONAL DEVICES – USING PERSPECTIVE

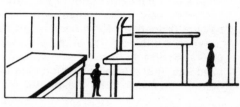

Scale distortion

The entire setting is built with everything proportionally scaled up or down, to produce dwarfs or giants.

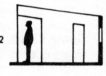

False perspective

Only strictly accurate from one viewpoint, the false perspective may be localised or overall, to increase the illusion of depth and extent.
1, Perspective is seen on a flat scenic plane which may be photographic or painted by an artist; 2, Progressive perspective change in set construction; 3, Perspective model background.

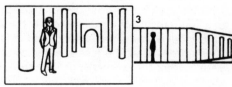

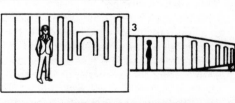

Scaled set dressing

By arranging larger set dressings in the foreground and smaller items in the distance, the illusions of space and extent are greatly enhanced.

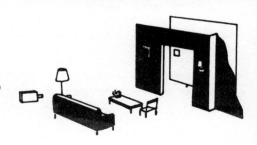

Staging Devices—Mirrors

Just as wall mirrors in the home can make a room appear more spacious, so too, appropriately used mirrors can enhance the studio setting. *Mirror shots* still have their popularity as a productional ploy, showing a foreground performer combined with the reflections of distant people.

Mirrors can present their embarrassing moments, though, for they have a propensity for reflecting offstage equipment, lights, and other unwanted subjects. By angling a mirror or tipping it downwards, it is often possible to 'lose' the unwanted reflections. The same approach is used with glass-faced wall pictures (a hidden roll of paper can be tucked behind the frame to tilt it slightly).

Increasing camera viewpoints

Mirrors enable cameras to obtain viewpoints that might otherwise prove impracticable or restrictive during a production. Overhead shots of cookery demonstrations, pianists and dance routines, are typical mirror applications. The camera itself can seldom get into comparable positions conveniently.

On the debit side, slung mirrors usually need to be quite large to be effective (e.g. over 6 ft×8 ft). They are liable to be heavy, are rather cumbersome to position precisely, and may shadow-off lighting for nearby subjects.

Surface-silvered plastic mirrors are fine for many applications where smaller units are required, or a distorted image effect needed (by twisting or bending mirror surface).

'Expanding space'

Shooting via a mirror can enable us to obtain a much longer shot of a set than studio space normally permits. In a small studio, the increase in effective camera-distance can prove an extremely useful facility. Any shoot-off at the top or sides of the shot may be masked off either with a foreground matte or vignette (e.g. a model theatre proscenium arch), an intermediate over-piece (cutting piece), and/or wings (pages 30, 90) or an electronically inserted surround (page 154).

Large wheeled mirrors (e.g. 10 ft×12 ft), of a type used for rear-projection set-ups can be adopted in staging. 'Corridors' have been constructed from facing mirrors. Multi-reflections offer an occasional decorative idea. Surprisingly effective results have been obtained too, by shooting through a peephole in a scenic backing onto a facing mirror, for the mirror doubles distance in a small staging area. Even a 'token' crowd scene has been doubled convincingly, using this trick.

CONSTRUCTIONAL DEVICES – MIRRORS

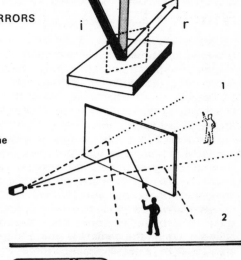

Basic laws of reflection

1, Light is reflected at an angle, (r) equal to the incident angle at which the light beam strikes the surface (i). The imaginary 'normal' plane is at right angles to the reflecting surface where the rays meet. The i, r, and 'normal' always lie in the same plane ; 2, The reflected image appears laterally reversed, and as far behind the mirror, as the subject is in front.

Changing the viewpoint with mirrors

3, Using a single overhead mirror, a laterally reversed, inverted image results ; 4, A similar reverse-angle shot ; 5, Using two mirrors, resulting in a top shot ; 6, A separate two-mirror periscope produces a high angle shot ; 7, A portable periscope stand or camera attachment permits a low angle shot.

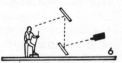

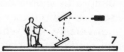

From the beginning, economics govern developments.

Economics—Initial Considerations

Production costs are really embryonic in the initial script and its presentation concepts. Certain subjects lend themselves to a range of staging interpretations. Others are inherently cheap (e.g. interviews) or costly (e.g. convincing battle scenes). Good simple staging is preferable to unnecessary elaboration. Some presentations over-reach and provide 'sawn-off' economy versions of situations that need large-scale approaches if they are to be tackled at all.

Production demands have to be kept within the facilities and budget available. To achieve this, one may have to resort to a script rewrite (e.g. omitting or relocating scenes) or use restricted settings (e.g. pages 74, 76) or, perhaps, introduce stock location film shots ('library shots') use rear projection, chroma key, or some similar stratagem.

Few shows lay equal emphasis upon each scene or sequence within them. It is better to concentrate expenditure upon a longer-duration scene in which the camera is going to get good pictorial value from the staging than a lesser scene where an abbreviated treatment would suffice. This is obvious in principle, but is not always easy in practice.

Directing techniques
Ideally, staging effort should be intrinsically related to the director's camera treatment. However, while some directors can anticipate each shot precisely, and have settings developed to suit this treatment, many more cannot visualise or commit themselves to this degree. Instead, they have the set designer provide an appropriate type of environment (with any specific features the script calls for), and then dispose their performers around this setting, selecting their final versions on camera in the studio. Some set designers find themselves, therefore, 'selling' good shots, action moves and visual opportunities, rather than working to a director's specified pictorial requirements. But these ideas must be practicable for camera, sound and lighting treatment.

The camera segments the scene
It is all too easy to devise staging that looks magnificent as a whole, in a distant view, but when shot mostly from closer viewpoints appears as little more than 'poles growing out of performers' heads'! Staging should be attractive, meaningful, effective, in the segmented shots the viewer sees. It is possible to spend time, effort and money on devising delightful scenic and lighting effects that the camera is never going to see, as the director is concentrating on other aspects of the scene. But, conversely, one would be ill-advised to limit the staging to the absolute minimum anticipated when planning the production. A telling cross-shot added during rehearsal may shoot off and reveal the studio walls. Some leeway is clearly necessary. Evidently, close coordination is the foundation of economic staging.

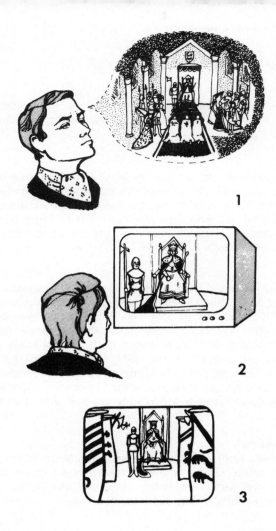

Staging economics

1, Above all, the TV designer has to be a realist. There is little point in working in terms outside the budget and facilities ; 2, The result can be a rather pathetic, truncated version ; 3, But even simplified staging can be improved with certain changes and little extra expense. Here, banners border the picture, masking its edges. Cut-outs of weapons (even of people !) are silhouetted.

Economics— Cost Saving

The staging opportunities of smaller TV studios are necessarily restricted. But many achieve minor miracles, nevertheless, by ingenious presentation economies.

Neutral settings
In small studios extensive use can be made of multi-purpose neutral staging areas (pages 110, 112). These offer considerable flexibility at low cost. Lighting can be used to change background tones or introduce decorative shapes and patterns (pages 114, 120). Supplementary decoration can be added in the form of cut-outs, drapes, screens and panels and stock units (pages 30, 32, 122, 126-134).

Cheap materials
Where the television staging has once-only usage, especially if it is being devised in situ, cheap, flimsy, utility materials can often be applied provided little handling is involved. Cardboard (strawboard) can be stapled to a light wooden framework, taped into tubular shapes. Designs may be stencilled or colour-shaded with aerosol spray paint. Adhesive decorative tapes (colour, metallic) can transform surfaces. Staple-guns (staple hammers) enable fabric to be stapled to standard flats, as an overall covering, pleated, or arranged as drapes. Lightweight modular units of prepared board are readily reused, and dismantled for storage.

Simplified treatment
You can often provide entirely realistic effects in a surprisingly short time by applying quite simple surface treatments. Predecorated sheeting (plastic, wallpaper) provides new or weathered brick, masonry, dry-stone walling, tiling, woodgrains, etc.

Quick scenic changes
The appearance of a setting may be changed rapidly by such devices as turn-over two colour Venetian blinds, turn-round screens with alternative decoration, pull-away sets, drop-in drapes, lighting changes and so on.

Indirect approaches
Perhaps the most important consideration in low-budget staging is to avoid pretentiousness. Rather than use a poor staging substitute and risk a tatty, amateurish result, it is better not to attempt direct imitation in the studio, but to tackle the project more obliquely. Limbo treatment is an extreme example (page 110), but partial settings (74, 76), an abstract approach or electronic picture insertion (page 154) may produce a more interesting, effective audience impact.

STAGING ECONOMICS – COST SAVING

Revamping

The same plain-walled three-fold set has been used here throughout. The only changes made are, in general, set dressings and some basic scenic aspects. Re-lighting can introduce further modifications. 1, Dummy fireplace ; 2, Dummy doorway ; 3, Venetian blind ; 4, Mirror ; 5, Drapes (on batten) ; 6, Drapes with ninon short curtain (on batten).

Economies—Box and Shell Modulars

As we have seen, certain structural facilities are regularly required in TV staging. If these can be provided in a form that is easily stored, and most important, can be readily modified or refurbished, then they offer very considerable economies.

Box units

Box units are reminiscent of giant play bricks. They can be made from hardboard (prepared board) or plywood facings, which fasten on to a cubic frame. Faces can be clipped or screwed on to this foundation, and changed or redecorated to suit the requirements of individual shows. Plastic surface sheeting and edge-trims of plastic or metal add to the durability of the box. They may be stored in complete or in dismantled form.

The box units can be used singly, or arranged to build up into tables or benches for displays or demonstrations. A selection of sizes and shapes adds to their versatility. Square, rectangular, and drum forms have the widest applications.

Even such a simple expedient as having unit faces finished with different tones, can introduce interesting design and pattern variants. Conversely, similarly toned surfaces can be aligned to provide a continuous plane of a single tonal value.

Shell units

Shell units are ostensibly similar, except that one or more faces are removed to provide knee-room and tuck-away storage for sundries during a show (e.g. utensils for a cookery demonstration).

Structurally weaker than box units, shells are also less suitable for stacking or for constructing built-up structures. However, they have the merit of enabling people to sit at them, either as isolated or combined 'desks', for quizzes, interviews, panel discussions, etc.

While round or semi-circular shapes have fewer applications, cubic or wedge-shaped units can provide a useful variety of scenic presentations.

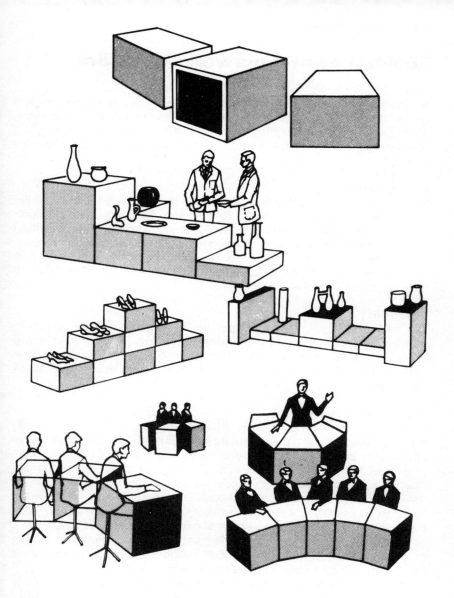

STAGING ECONOMIES

Box units
Variations in shape and size provide flexibility of use. Facing board or card can be used to hide joins.

Shell units
Being hollow at one end, shell units can be used as tables, desks, benches. Wedge-shaped units form horseshoe configurations.

Economies—Framework Modulars

Smaller, general purpose studios usually have the combined problem of low budgets, little storage space, and limited facilities. For them, any device that increases the variety and flexibility of their staging, is a valuable asset. The *framework unit* is a modular fitting of considerable versatility.

Construction
Fundamentally devised as 'construction kits', framework units employ slotted angle-iron lengths, or are formed from square or round section metal tubes welded into rectangular elements. These in turn can then be bolted or slotted together into wedges, cubes, or rectangular shapes. Their inherent strength enables these elements to be conjoined into units up to several feet long. Cross-members join units together to form complete modules.

Versatility
The modules have many applications as screens, tables, benches, shelving, structural units, even as lightweight rostra. A range of standard sized boards faced with a selection of materials can be slipped or screwed to the module frames to devise totally-clad box shapes, or to allow partly clad arrangements.

Surface treatment
Looking more closely at these attached boards, it is apparent that they can provide almost inexhaustible opportunities: They may serve as drawing panels ie: blackboards, steel-based boards (for attaching magnetic-strip items) or plastic-coated panels for tacky-back graphics. They may be used as plain surfaces of selected tone and hue (solid, translucent, transparent), as decorative panels (with ornamental motifs, clip-on fabric or texture sheets), as chroma-key panels (e.g. blue surfaces for electronic insertion of captions or graphics (page 154), or as display panels for maps, graphics, photo enlargements, station or programme identification symbol (Logos). Low castored stands can be attached to units to increase their mobility.

Particularly in smaller general purpose studios, metal frame units can be re-jigged to suit the varied requirements of individual programmes in a comparatively short time, while reducing the need for extensive stock or storage space.

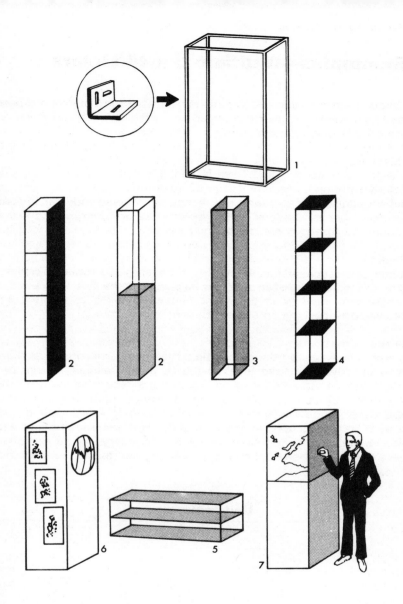

STAGING ECONOMIES

Framework modulars

1, From a simple demountable framework structure, a variety of units can be built; They may be; 2, Surface-clad, to provide decorative structures of closed or 3, open form; 4, Vertical shelf unit; 5, Horizontal shelves; 6, An enclosed pillar-unit with internally illuminated panels and programme logo or station identification symbol; 7, Similar pillar-unit with magnetic map, and Chroma-key panel.

67

Economies—Multiple Use of Units

Although stock scenic units are usually created for a familiar purpose, they may sometimes be transformed with little or no alteration for an entirely different, scenic role.

Flats
The narrow flats (1, 1½, 2 ft wide and 9 ft high) used to form jogs (returns) in normal settings (page 52) can be adapted as shelving, or laid on edge to hide ground row lamps, or coupled together to form square columns, besides their applications in constructing cattle troughs, enclosed girders and ceiling beams.

Arches
A standard scenic arch may be filled in to serve as a recessed shelving unit. The top section of an arch may be placed on the ground to simulate a basement window at pavement (sidewalk) level, or inverted and decorated to become an ancient throne.

Transformations
A pair of fully-glazed doors may be turned in to a decorative skylight. Wooden dowelling used for prison bars, or the railings in front of a house, can be placed on their side as part of a decorative room-divider. A profiled flat that normally contains a window plug (page 24) may, when the window is removed, be fitted with a translucent display screen. Transformations of this kind endow the same scenic unit with new, wider, uses saving the construction of a new piece (which might have only limited productional applications) and extending the scope of existing stock.

Unit conversion

Feet ←	metres · feet →	Metres
3·28	1	0·304
6·561	2	0·609
9·842	3	0·914
13·12	4	1·219
16·4	5	1·524
19·68	6	1·828
22·96	7	2·133
26·24	8	2·438
29·52	9	2·743
32·28	10	3·04

DESIGN ECONOMIES

Multiple use of units

Individual scenic units can be utilised in various ways.
1, Two glazed French doors can be end-joined to provide a long wall-window, or a ceiling-light; 2, Simple cross-braced wooden rods can be used as railings, window-bars, or a decorative grille; 3, An arch-head, can be turned into a low window, or even a throne; 4, An arch can be in-filled to become a bookcase or a window unit.

69

Economies—Multi-Use of Settings

If the same setting can be re-used during a programme to present a fresh look to the viewer, we are clearly making extremely desirable savings— in money, space, and often in time.

There are several approaches to the multi-use of staging. All offer interesting opportunities:

Re-angled camera viewpoints
Simplest of all, is to have cameras shoot the scene from several directions, when with appropriate anticipation, the scene can be made to appear quite different. This technique is really confined to static closer shots, where the camera takes in only part of the background at a time from any given viewpoint. (This same principle, incidentally, enables us to re-use a photo-backing several times, by ensuring that different segments of it are visible on each occasion.)

Lighting treatment
Lighting treatment may be used to modify the appearance of staging. Even a simple plain cyc can be relit in many ways (pages 114-120).

Revamping
Revamping can alter the entire character or location of a scene. It takes either of two forms:
1. Scenic units are repositioned to create new compositional arrangements, also termed 'cheating'.
2. Set dressings are modified or replaced, furniture is repositioned or substituted (page 62). This method provides considerable flexibility. Dummy architectural features (e.g. fireplaces, doors, windows) can be changed, drapes can be replaced (even reversed), wall furnishings are easily altered (maps, pictures, venetian blinds that imply windows). Even as slight a change as having drapes open or closed, replacing dummy book-backs in a bookcase, introducing floral displays, hanging different wall pictures or moving a room-divider unit, can substantially alter the look of a setting. The method is often referred to as *re-dressing*.

Trucking
Trucking (wheeled platform, float, stage wagon). A small setting or part of a scene can be wheeled into place or moved around for the camera. Quite simple devices such as turning the foreground mobile unit round can transform the picture (page 84).

Changing backgrounds
Rear Projection (page 152) or *electronic picture insertion* (page 154) enables one to switch the entire scenic background instantaneously.

STAGING ECONOMIES – MULTIPLE USE OF SETS

Different viewpoints
A change in camera position can provide a new pictorial effect.

Revamping
Just four identical columns, yet simple repositioning gives the picture new visual appeal. When coupled with lighting changes, striking variations become possible.

Economies— Permanent Sets

Many productions have to have fresh staging for each presentation to accommodate new subject material, to satisfy varying treatment and to enhance their audience appeal. But to continually devise new staging for each programme is an expensive practice, wasteful of resources.

The regular setting

Certain shows actually gain from the continued use of a regular setting. The audience recognises it and associates the look with that particular production. The *permanent set* gives a sense of cohesion and continuity to a series. The permanent set may, of course, be a *composite* (page 20), selected sections of which are erected in the studio for a specific day's requirements.

For many smaller studio units, a further approach to the permanent set has proved invaluable. Here, the same staging set-up remains built in the studio for a long period, but is systematically modified to suit the needs of each individual show. Part of the actual studio may be specially designed for this purpose.

Changeable features

This custom-built area can be altered in a number of ways, including :
Wall surfaces—These can be arranged to be reversed, slid, inverted, covered . . . to alter their shade, pattern, texture, shape, contouring, etc.
Changeable drapes—These can be of reversible material, and used fully pleated or stretched, to conceal all or parts of the background.
Translucent panels—Provided as 'windows', decorative or architectural features, the panels can be rear-lit in various ways, display shadows, abstract motifs, etc. (page 122).
Lighting treatment—Lighting changes offer variations in the background tone, or hue. Textural features can be emphasised or suppressed. Light distribution and pattern can be readily altered (pages 114-120).
Chroma key (*C.S.O.*)—Panels of suitable tone or colour (usually blue or yellow) can be introduced into the background to serve as a keying or switching area for electronic insertion. The resulting display screens can be used to present captions, graphics of all kinds, and for live, filmed or video-taped action.

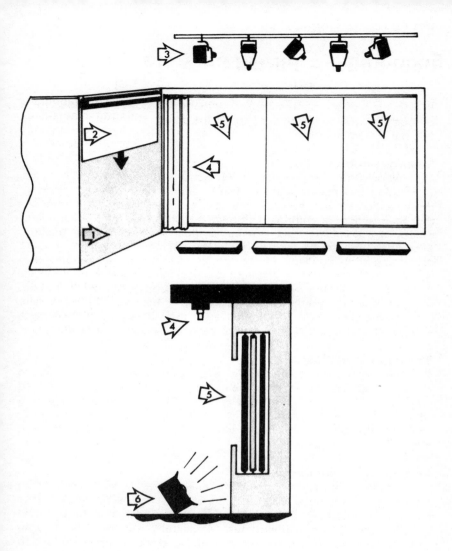

STAGING ECONOMIES – PERMANENT SETS

Suggested permanent small studio set-up
A highly adaptable design with :
1, Electronic insertion keying background (Chroma-key) ; 2, Roll-blind
backgrounds ; 3, Projected backgrounds and patterns ; 4, Adjustable reversible
drapes ; 5, Hook-in, slide-along, double-sided wall panels (neutrals, wood
finish, front-projection screens, translucent panels, Chroma-key background,
etc.) ; 6, Ground lamps (trough, strip-lights, cyc lights).

73

Economies— Partial Sets

If a fraction of the simulated environment will convey the idea for a production, why build it larger? This is the design philosophy underlying the use of *partial sets*.

Selective abbreviation
Originating from necessity, from crowded studios and low budgets, TV staging has made extensive use of partial sets. Strictly speaking, most studio settings, however realistic, can be said to be 'partial', in that they seldom attempt to reproduce a replica of a total environment unless of a domestic room interior, a small shop, or similar location. Even then, the fourth wall is generally excluded. But here we are discussing the concept of designing staging in an abbreviated sectionalised form, as a segment of the scene, complete in every important detail. Thus we see the porch of a house, but nothing more. A ticket office represents the entire foyer of a theatre. All the requisite features are there, within a limited area. Judiciously positioned parts suggest that the setting is much more extensive than it really is.

The combined illusion
We can convey the impression of a quayside scene by including in our shot a surface that imitates the hull of a ship, perhaps with reflected water-ripple, a bollard and coils of rope. The associated background sounds of cranes, hooting tugs, water lapping and screaming gulls, complete the illusion. In a night scene, lighting localises visibility and helps to curtail staging.

Anticipatory planning needed
If carefully controlled, partial sets enable the scenic designer to achieve considerable elaboration and variety. This is particularly true where a large number of scenes are required, and larger settings would be impracticable or superfluous. Unskilfully introduced, though, partial sets can result in over-restriction and lead to a cramped production which lacks performer movement. Directors who rely largely upon their intuitive judgment by setting-up shots through the camera rather than careful anticipatory planning, can find this type of staging technique inhibiting, for it gives little opportunity for diversifying shots especially at the last minute.

Sky-cloth

Hedge
Unit

Fibre-glass
Tree-trunk

Fence section

STAGING ECONOMIES – PARTIAL SETS

Small sections
The environment can be implied by building up just a small section of the
location. If the shot is to be restricted, then only as much need be provided as the
camera sees. The scene looks complete, within the shot.

Larger sets
Where the camera is to take various shots, or several viewpoints are intercut, or
action is more fluid, a more complete treatment becomes necessary.

75

Conveying the essence of a situation.

Economies— Selected Elements

By using just a few carefully chosen features it is often possible to recapture the 'feel' of an entire locale with surprising conviction. Thus a realistic illusion can be built up with these *selected elements* in such a way that the actual sparsity of the staging is quite overlooked. The effect can be naturalistic or abstract, according to the particular aspects that are chosen, and how they are shot.

Degrees of brevity
Let us look at one fundamental example. Suppose that in a fairly localised shot (e.g. 12×9 ft area) the camera shows someone leaning on a horizontal bar, backed only by a plain grey flat. If the story line, dialogue and sound effects have caused us to interpret this as a ship at sea, then that is what it becomes. Where the ship's rail looks authentic and lifebelts and other maritime equipment is visible, the same scene may have added conviction. But often, quite restricted visual clues may suffice.

Clearly, we have to be perceptive in making our selection. The viewer could hardly be expected to interpret a couple of volumes on a shelf as being the interior of a bookshop. But if appropriate posters are attached to a flat behind the assistant, and the shadows of lettering on the shop window cast across it, then it can be readily accepted that this is the premises of *'John Doe, Bookseller'*. The fact that these shadows actually originate from a slide projector is immaterial.

The potentialities of lighting
Sometimes an effect can be devised just as well by lighting treatment as by scene units. Lighting can suggest that a performer is near a window, if a window shadow from a slide, stencil or cut-out, is projected on to him, or if the shadow of a real offstage window unit that is never seen falls across him. Alternatively, the scene can be shot through an actual part of the set such as a window unit which has been placed in the foreground.

Associative light patterns can be used realistically, or as an abstract design.

If the shadows of a leafy branch are cast across someone standing by a 'brick' flat, the result is realistic. If the same branch is used to form patterns on a translucent screen, the result may be interpreted as either real or decorative, according to the situation. Again, a branch might be made to form elongated straggling shadows across a red cyclorama, so that this natural object now provides an abstract design.

STAGING ECONOMIES –
SELECTED ELEMENTS
Scenic economy

The greatest economy is possible by using only the minimum of scenic elements. But these must be unambiguous.

A park bench (against black drapes) can convey the idea of a nocturnal park scene – but the viewer must recognise it instantly as such.

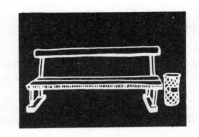

Approached to selection

1, A bookshop location could be created by using a very complete, extensively-dressed setting. Photo-backing, rear-projection or electronic insertion, are the only economic TV studio methods for this approach ; 2, Too few visual clues, and the result is unconvincing ; 3, By restricting the shot with suitable foreground pieces, one can provide greater subjectivity ; 4, Relatively few scenic elements are needed to conjure an environment – particularly where the lighting itself is highly selective and localised, and much of the setting falls into shadow.

Skeletal Staging

Essentially decorative, skeletal staging treatments have a deceptively simple appearance, yet often epitomise the very essence of design abstraction.

In its simplest form, skeletal design is created by suspending isolated motifs—a group of cartwheels, perhaps, or representational cut-outs. Vertical poles may be grouped to provide compositional centres. Hung streamers, ropes, nets, whitened bare tree branches, wire-work and lanterns, are typical ingredients of this imaginative spatial decor. Coupled with sympathetic lighting design, powerful effects can be produced for musical and dance presentations.

Standard architectural units can play their part in skeletal settings, either as sections of a decorative assembly or as isolated pieces abstracted from a total environment. An example of the former is the stylised 'artist's garret' set that includes the essential architectural and environmental features, embellished for dramatic effect.

Isolated units can be positioned against a neutral background, enabling us to fabricate an entire room in the imagination. This stimulating (and very economical!) staging approach has been used over a wide field of programmes such as plays, talks, discussions, recitals and comedy sketches.

Structural anatomy

The most ingenious approach to skeletal staging is expressed through what might be termed 'structural anatomy'. Here, an environment is re-created by building appropriate frameworks, and attaching to them representative profiled areas. Emphasis is on outline and construction. In architectural subjects, the effect results from such associative elements as windows, doors, balconies, staircases, balustrades.

Most subjects can be stylised for skeletal purposes, often in a variety of ways. Forest trees might be suggested effectively by block outlines, by tracery with symbolised suggestion of foliage or by abstracted shapes.

Design for the camera treatment

Skeletal staging imaginatively explores the screen's visual opportunities. But many of its effects are realised only in longer shots. Moreover, the result may only be really successful from certain viewpoints. In closer shots, there is the danger that pictures may resolve themselves into little more than 'sticks growing out of peoples' heads'. Certainly, the total decorative impact tends to be lost, unless the staging is deliberately conceived to be broken up into self-effective sections.

A staging method that is sometimes misleadingly referred to as 'skeletal', uses simple line-drawings on plain flattage, to provide large scale graphics, or cartoon sketches—usually for comedy or children's programmes.

SKELETAL STAGING

Staging variations
1, Suspended isolated units (symbolised cartwheels) provide decorative design ;
2, Abstraction here uses real scenic units isolated from their total environment ;
3, Geometric construction in wood, metal tubing, stretched wire, rope, etc.,
create attractive patterns ; 4, Skeletal staging here relies upon abstraction from a
stylised architectural style ; 5, Silhouetted construction suggests a specific type
of location, for a dance sequence ; 6, The amusing caricature produced by
skeletal simplification, could with different presentation become bizarre and
nightmarish.

Space Problems— Multi-Use of Space

In small studios, space is at a premium and so we may find it advantage-
ous to re-use the same staging area over and over again in the course
of a show. There are a number of well-tried methods that can help us
here. All have their merits and shortcomings, but have proved useful.

Flat backgrounds

'Flat' backgrounds can be provided by packs, drop-ins, reflex projection (page 152) or electronic picture insertion (page 154). They all
have the disadvantage that the camera can only, at most, track or zoom
to and from subject and background. It can not move sideways (crab,
truck), elevate, depress, or shoot obliquely to the scene without
spoiling the illusion.

Packs are formed by stacking a series of flat backgrounds. These
may be decorated, scenic or photographic flats. Removing the top flat
from the pile reveals the next beneath. For maximum coverage, the
backgrounds should have a 4 : 3 format and be of similar sizes.

Backgrounds can also be *dropped in* or *flown out*. The simplest
technique uses a series of scenic cloths or hessian-backed photo
blow-ups, which can be unrolled, one over the next. Where ceiling
space allows, rigid backings can be used, and hoisted (flown) in and
out. This last technique is sometimes used to clear selected staging
from the studio floor and provide more space for camera operations.
In this way entire settings can be flown and dropped-in by electric
hoists or counter-balanced roof-lines (scenic lines). Very high ceilings
(flies) are necessary for this purpose.

Adaptable forms

Folding flats. In this arrangement, hinged flats can be opened up to
reveal a new scene on their reverse. The resulting three-fold assembly
can be dressed and furnished, to form a set to be shot from all angles.

Nesting sets. Here one scene is set-up completely within another,
larger setting. After use, this inner staging is struck (removed) and
cameras set up on the outer decor, which has been dressed in advance.
Both sets offer full productional opportunities.

Reversible scenery. Occasionally, one can transform staging by
using a reversible unit. A wheeled set can, for example, be designed
to show a new, different location on its rear side.

Revamping, or repositioning the cameras (pages 58, 66) offer
further opportunities to extend area use, as do *mobile units* (page 84).

Reflex projection (axial front projection), *rear projection* (page 152)
and *electronically inserted backgrounds* (page 154) undoubtedly
provide the greatest flexibility for rapid background changes, although
necessarily bounded by the single camera presentation limits of all
flat background systems.

Packs
Individually decorated flats are laid in a pile, the top flat being removed to reveal the next underneath.

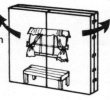

Folding flats
Hinged open to show the new scene. In this pantomime example, little set dressing or furniture is used. Most of it is painted on the background ! The method can be used equally well for realistic settings.

Nesting sets
Placed one within the other, the inner set is struck to reveal the outer. The lighting however, must be arranged either as a compromise to suit both sets simultaneously ; or as two juxtaposed set-ups, creating more complex, congested rigging.

Reversible scenery
A low wheeled truck contains the interior of a Victorian police station. But reversed, the camera sees part of an elegant drawing room.

Space Problems— Mobile Sections

Where the open side of a box set is too narrow or restricted for every camera access, or where we want to create a temporary extension to the acting area, several useful staging tricks can be introduced.

Movable units

Swinger (*flipper*). Flats forming part of the walls of a setting can be edge-hinged—open to provide camera entry, closed to appear as a continuous wall surface in shots from other cameras. The lower edge of this type of swinger may have a support wheel to allow quick, quiet re-positioning. Downstage walls of settings are quite often made to swing in this way. This enables cameras to move up into the set, allows cross shooting (particularly when side walls of the set have not been splayed) or even provides masking for reverse-angle shots.

Gallows arm. This is a light horizontal batten from which a drape can be hung, usually to extend a side wall. Fixed at one end to an adjacent flat or scenic unit, this device allows cameras to gain admittance to an acting area and may be used to prevent shoot-off on reverse-angle shots (page 90). It has the advantage that it can be repositioned very quickly and silently. If hinged, the gallows-arm can be angled readily (page 32). An alternative arrangement is a fixed gallows-arm on which a track or a swag-cord is fitted to pull the drape aside when required.

Wild walls. These are scenic flats that are arranged to be removed easily during the production. Part of a side-wall in a box set may, for example, be shifted so that cameras and lights can approach action from a new direction. The wild wall may be *run* (i.e. lifted and man-handled) silently to a pack or storage position, or may be fitted with concealed wheels. Provided that there is sufficient headroom above the flat and that the lighting will not be shadowed, the wall can be flown out of the way of operations.

Floaters. Floaters are isolated scenic units that are moved for specific shots. They may provide a temporary plane, e.g. as a door-backing in an area of the studio floor required for camera tracking. They can introduce provisional scenery, to extend a set, or to imply its 'fourth wall'. A front door unit or a window unit often supplies a foreground piece beyond which the main staging area is visible. We do not see any more of the 'exterior of the house'.

Operational freedom

Movable sections of this kind allow freer camera and sound boom movement. Occasionally, quite large scenic sections (e.g. an entire shop front) may be wheeled aside to simplify continuous production. Where a camera has actually to track through a doorway or window, the unit is constructed in *break-through* form, the separate sections pulling aside as the camera moves through.

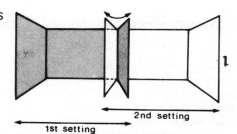

2nd setting

1st setting

Swinger's (**Flippers**)

1, The whole of a wall (double-faced) may be hinged to splay, and so provide better camera access; 2, Part of a wall may be hinged, for more flexible camera treatment, in flip in, or flip out forms.

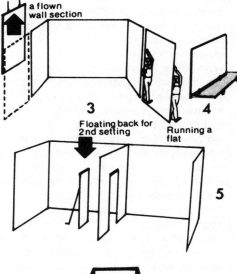

Flip in

Flip out

a flown wall section

Wild Walls (**Floats**)

3, Parts of the wall can be flown, or man-handled ('run') out of position; 4, A wheeled wall section.

Floating back for 2nd setting

Running a flat

Floaters

5, Where a backing is required only temporarily, it may be set in, and struck. Here, unrelated settings have been conjoined with a common door, to save space, the backing preventing shoot-through; 6, The foreground floater here contains a break-through street door to allow a camera to track through.

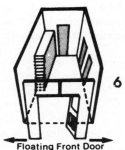

Floating Front Door

83

Space Problems— Mobile Units

Mobile units are usually small complete scenic areas that are totally mobile, and may be moved into position for just a few specific shots in the course of a show. The scenic alteration can be very localised, like the quick-change table tops that show 'before' and 'after' a meal, so suggesting the passage of time in a scene.

Mobile pieces can provide temporary foregrounds such as a wheeled-in desk, a floral display on a wheeled plinth, a set-in decorative screen for peep-through shots or even a wheeled hedge-unit (page 75, 107). These can be introduced and removed quickly to avoid baulking camera shots or moves.

Prepared staging
Wheeled low platforms (e.g. 9×12 ft) can be built up with the entire staging for a small scene, or part of a larger assembly. Known variously as *trucks, floats* or *stage wagons*, these mobile units may be wheeled in succession into the same staging area, perhaps with a rear-projection screen or chroma key keying surface (pages 152, 154), to provide a variety of backgrounds. The same group of lamps, too, may service each scene in turn.

The main drawback to large mobile units is generally the amount of repositioning and parking space required by the trucks before and after use. However, particularly where the scenes make full use of chroma-key and the trucked staging is minimal, the results can outweigh this limitation.

Although for very basic staging a truck would be unnecessarily cumbersome, for example, where only a couple of chairs and a table are required, for more complicated or fully-dressed inserts (i.e. all properties and set dressings in position) the ready-prepared assembly saves valuable time.

Large areas
Really large mobile areas can permit whole sections of an orchestra, or an audience, to be repositioned during a show, to give variety in presentation and layout. Powered by electric motors—but more usually by strong stagehands—the units may prove unwieldy and noisy to move unless properly designed for the purpose.

SPACE PROBLEMS – MOBILE UNITS

Unit flexibility

Mobile platforms are invaluable where staging is to be repositioned and where loose material such as 'snow', 'sand' is involved.

Where a number of separate articles such as furniture or other props would take time to transport and arrange, the platform allows repositioning.

A small completely trucked setting may be positioned before a cyc, backdrop, or chroma-key backing, and subsequently moved to a storage area in the studio.

Shooting Freedom— Variety of Shots

The shape of a studio setting can modify the potential range and variety of shots available. Settings that are narrow or deep, restrict cameras to more or less front-on positions. Most close-up action in the upstage areas then has to be shot from downstage on lenses with a narrow angle of view. Such a lens has the disadvantage of seeming to reduce relative distances. Moreover, the highly magnified image makes camera movement more obvious.

Camera access
Sets are often arranged with the side walls splayed out to give better opportunities for cameras to move into the setting. Foreground furniture is invariably kept to a minimum in continuous TV production (or moved when out of shot), where upstage camera access is needed. However, it is often neither practicable, nor environmentally realistic, to stage all scenes with the 'decks cleared for action' in this way. Many real locations are relatively confined, cluttered places and if we build studio replicas (even a simple office set) that are unnaturally furnitureless, just to provide plenty of space for camera movement, the impression on the screen will lack conviction.

Camera peepholes
One solution to allow shot variety, is to construct the scene with all the required features, and to circumvent any obstacles by providing peepholes through which the cameras can shoot otherwise inaccessible parts of the acting area. Even when a setting has been generally designed for effective camera access, this can widen the scope for shots.

The simplest arrangement, of course, is to use a door or window in the side of the set for peep-through shots. Cameras can also shoot through removable fireplace-backs, through pull-aside drapes, through *camera traps* in the form of sliding or hinged wall panels and, through wall holes concealed by hung pictures or similar devices.

It may be feasible to move drapes or flats (pages 32, 82) aside to enable the cameras to see the action.

Further methods
It is frequently practicable to design the setting so that scenic features hide cameras and so allow them to achieve certain viewpoints. A wall-section, buttress, ornamental screen or hedge have proved valuable for this purpose. Walls can be constructed with *returns* or *breaks* (page 52), to permit shoot-through positions for cameras behind the staging.

Mirrors, too, can sometimes increase shooting freedom (page 58) and enable a camera to reach angles that would otherwise prove impractical.

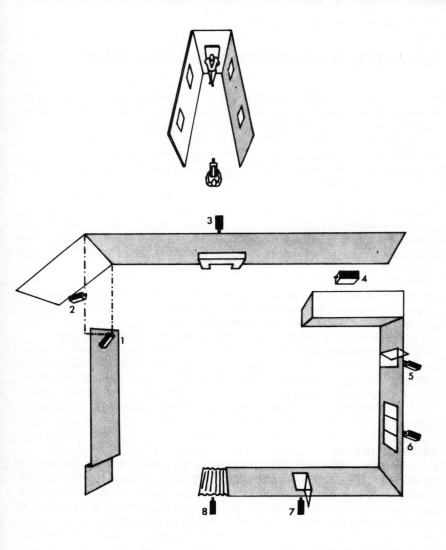

SHOOTING FREEDOM – VARIETY OF SHOTS

Shape of setting
Narrow sets restrict camera access, action, and lighting treatment.

Camera peepholes
In this unlikely example, all the typical methods of incorporating camera peepholes in a setting have been included.
1, Gap in wall return ; 2, Swinger ; 3, Through-fireplace shot ; 4, Hidden camera ;
5, Shooting through door ; 6, Shooting through window ; 7, Wall trap (camera trap) e.g. hinged wall picture ; 8, Pull-aside drapes.

Shooting Freedom—Shooting Over

In shows of any complexity, cameras may shoot past the confines of the setting and reveal lamps and the studio beyond. We can anticipate this happening in certain common circumstances:

1. Where the flattage height is too low relative to the distance of the camera from it, particularly when wide-angle lenses are in use.

2. When the camera elevation is low (e.g. below about 3 ft) or the camera tilts upwards.

3. When a subject is placed higher than the camera lens position (particularly when close), or if a camera looks up to people on rostra, staircases, balconies, etc.

In these situations where the camera shoots over the set, either the shot must be modified, or the staging altered in some way.

Topping-up

When the designer has left an insufficient safety area for the intended shot, or the director has revised his camera angle, it may be necessary to *top-up* the far walls by increasing their height with additional vertical flattage. But taller flats are not always a rational solution.

In smaller studios the height of the ceiling (and, hence, of all staging) is limited, anyway. Even where high flats are feasible, the steeper vertical lighting angles that result tend to debase lighting treatment and so degrade picture quality. Tall flats are often quite inappropriate, too, for the scale of a setting. A small cottage room with walls some fifteen feet high is unlikely to look convincing.

Masking pieces

An effective subterfuge that overcomes the need for high flattage is to provide an intermediate *masking piece* (overpiece, teaser, cutting piece) for the problem shot. This is a vertical plane introduced into the upper part of the picture, which prevents the camera seeing over the distant setting. Devised in the form of a fascia, arch, overhanging beam, etc., this usually appears as a natural-looking architectural feature. Remember that quite small low masking pieces nearer the camera have a similar effect to larger surfaces further away.

Ceilings

In more extreme cases, cameras may only be prevented from shooting over walls by introducing horizontal or sloping ceilings despite their adverse influence on lighting treatment (page 94).

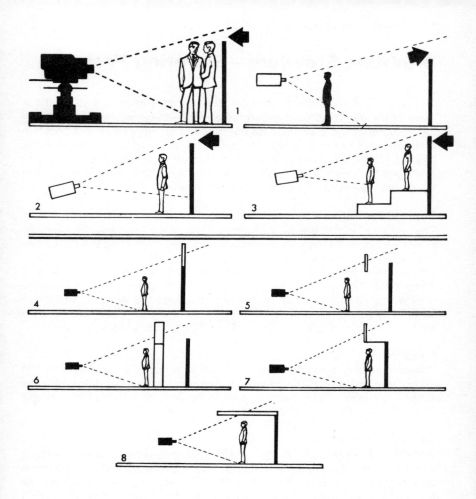

SHOOTING FREEDOM

Shooting over

1, Where the background is of insufficient height, the camera may shoot over, even on close shots on a level camera, with an average lens angle. Further from the background the likelihood increases ; 2, Low cameras shoot over very easily ; 3, Cameras at normal height are likely to shoot over when subjects are elevated.

Preventatives

4, Use higher flats or top-up flats ; 5, Use intermediate vertical masking pieces in the top of the shot ; 6, Use an intermediate architectural feature (e.g. an arch, or doorway in a wall) ; 7, Introduce a fascia ; 8, Introduce a ceiling.

The shot that reveals too much.

Shooting Freedom—Shooting Past

As cameras move from a position front-on to the setting, and shoot more obliquely in acutely angled cross-shots, they become increasingly liable to shoot off, past the side limits of the staging area. This problem is most likely to occur where the set is constructed in a shallow form, has no side walls, or is L-shaped. It also often arises when a director positions his cameras upstage and shoots back towards the imaginary fourth wall, which is the open side of the setting.

Typical remedies
The predicament could be overcome by altering the shot. This would usually involve changing the camera position, switching to a narrower lens angle, or moving in to a closer viewpoint. Alternatively the shoot-off can be accommodated by introducing vertical masking elements of some kind. The simplest staging expedient is to lengthen the distant wall with an additional flat, probably angled into the set. This additional surface need not, in fact, always be of full height. Sometimes even a foreground ornamental screen may suffice to provide a safety margin.

Drapes
Where suitable, a simpler solution still is to position a drape at the end of the flat which the camera is shooting past. This drape may be suspended from a bar, fixed to a gallows arm, or attached to a drape frame (page 32).

Masking subjects
A different approach is to position some intermediate masking subject at the border of the picture, so preventing the camera from seeing past the edge of the setting. This may be an architectural feature such as a pillar or the edge of a wall or arch, or an environmental object such as a shop sign, a bush, a parked car. Even people can be used for this purpose—a foreground waiter in a restaurant, a passer-by chatting in a street scene.

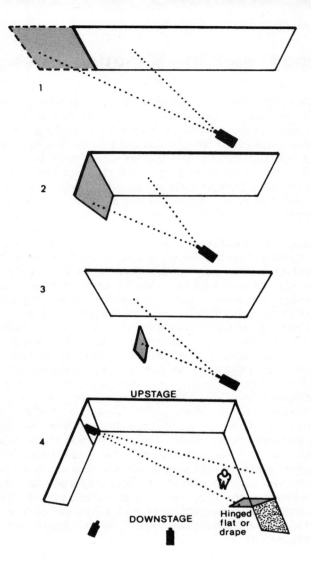

SHOOTING FREEDOM

Shooting past

Shallow staging occupies little floor space and readily allows packing and nesting. As cross shots easily shoot off, we may have to 1, extend the set ; 2, return the wall ; 3, introduce a masking piece.

When upstage cameras shoot downstage action, a downstage swinger or gallows arm, 4, may be necessary to prevent shoot-off.

Shooting Freedom—Shooting Through

Staging is usually planned so that the camera sees what is intended, and no more. Wherever openings of any sort are included in a setting we have to ensure that the camera does not accidentally shoot through them and reveal the studio beyond. So we introduce *scenic backings* of some kind to restrict the shot and obscure what is outside the confines of the staging. The commonest forms of backings are cyc cloths, painted scenic cloths (drops, backcloths), photographic enlargements, scenic flats and drapes. In addition to this application, they provide a visual extension to the setting, and may suggest a location (page 108).

The mechanics of backings

In purely mechanical terms, we must ensure that any backing really does mask off the scenic opening from all camera angles. If the backing is too small, too oblique, badly positioned, or too far away from the opening, cameras may shoot past it. If placed too close to the opening—a temptation in crowded studios—it might not be practicable to light the backing correctly overall, and extraneous shadows are liable to fall upon it (e.g. a street scene backing upon which window shadows are cast from a lit interior set). Side masking pieces such as brick-wall flats can allow a small backing to be used outside a large scenic opening.

Door backings

Doorways normally require backings indicating a corridor, hall or room beyond. But where space precludes this, the door in a side wall can usually be hinged to open into the room from the downstage side of the opening, or from the upstage side if it is to open outwards. This simple expedient prevents the camera shooting through when the door is opened. However, when a door is to be used that is positioned directly opposite the camera, the only methods of avoiding backings are to cheat the action (so that the performer is seen just closing the door as we cut to him) or to have the door opened only sufficiently for the performer to sidle in.

Photo backings

Photographic backings are initially relatively costly, but have the merit that they can be altered in various ways. Detail can be retouched, added, obliterated or emphasised quite readily. Monochrome photo blow-ups can be coloured by dye-retouching, to achieve results that are more convincing and flexible than an expensive coloured enlargement.

Stored on a wooden roller core, or stuck to a flat, a photo backing may be re-used effectively by repositioning (to reveal a previously unseen area), by masking-off part of it (foliage, bushes, wall, etc.), by retouching, sometimes by relighting (shading, colour, rear illumination. Rigid transluscent photo-panels are effective, but inevitably expensive.

92

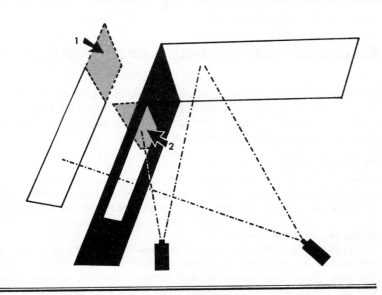

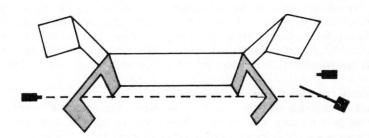

SHOOTING FREEDOM

Shooting through

Wherever there are openings in a setting, the camera is liable to shoot through and beyond.

The normal solution, as for Camera 1, is to provide a backing. But notice that in this example the backing is insufficient, so that Camera 2 shoots through, nevertheless.

Consequently, a large backing 1, a return 2, or masking (even closing the drapes slightly, may help) would be needed for Camera 2.

In composite staging, cameras and sound booms working on one part of the setting may be seen through adjoining arches or windows, if masking has not been anticipated.

93

Ceilings—Structural Solutions

A ceiling can give an indefinably authentic look to a studio setting and the conviction that it is a complete entity. In purely practical terms, ceilings are a useful precaution against cameras shooting over the set. They serve as one alternative to tall flattage.

Problem ceilings

However, ceilings can introduce operational problems for both lighting and sound treatment. They may not only cause spurious shadowing, but can so limit light angles that these have to be arranged solely to circumvent the ceiling, rather than chosen to suit the action or the atmospheric needs.

Occasionally, ceilings present no real restriction. It may be quite practicable to light shots through windows, doors, or wall-breaks in the setting, or from lamps hidden behind furniture or scenic features. But for continuous action production, such approaches are often not feasible, and compromise treatment from slung lamps is the only possibility.

Sound quality can be considerably modified by low ceilings. The rather hollow, 'boxy', reverberant sound encountered under such a ceiling alters distinctly as a speaker moves out to the more open acoustics of an unceilinged region. The pronounced audible change may even destroy the environmental illusion built up in the picture.

Practical solutions

Partial ceilings can be provided by flats laid across a corner or the upstage area of a set. These, when seen on camera, suggest that the ceiling is much more extensive. Often surprisingly little is necessary to achieve this. Sometimes it is possible to carry a partial ceiling over the upstage area, and stop it within a few feet of its adjoining wall. This then enables upstage action and staging to be lit through the resulting gap.

Overhanging flats are a useful means of local treatment, to suggest sloping ceilings. The inward sloping walls of an attic can be constructed similarly, and provide insurance against shooting over. However, if the slope is so marked as to produce an appreciable overhang, this may in turn create its own operational problems.

Cutting pieces are vertical planes interrupting the upper part of the picture, and so preventing shoot-off. In certain 'environments', where beams, vaulting or girders are architecturally appropriate, they can be readily introduced—provided they do not impede the sound boom. In most situations, a vertical plane representing a fascia can be inserted effectively yet unobtrusively. To suggest thickness in the fascia, a shallow soffit can be provided by a simple horizontal board attached to its lower edge.

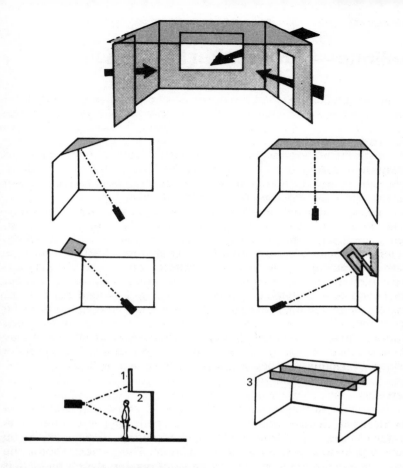

CEILINGS – STRUCTURAL SOLUTIONS

Total ceiling
Where scenic openings permit suitable lighting, a complete ceiling may be practicable. (Further lighting may be concealed behind staging and furniture.)

Partial ceilings (flat, level)
These can be used to prevent local shoot-off. They may impede lighting and cause spurious structural shadows.

Overhanging flats (sloping)
Precluding shoot-off with less lighting restriction. They are most suitable for attics and similar locations.

Cutting pieces
A cutting piece may be introduced as a vertical plane (e.g. a teaser), a structural or architectural feature (header, overhang, arch), a fascia 1, with a shallow soffit 2, to break the line. 3, Instead, a series of planes can be introduced to suggest beams or girders, so limiting shoot-off over a wide area, yet permitting lighting access.

95

Some ingenious ways of simulating ceilings require no construction.

Ceilings—Substitution Methods

Another staging approach to the provision of ceilings, is to sidestep the issue altogether, by providing a substitute in place of actual structures.

Background cloth

The most obvious example is where a scenic cloth or photo blow-up displays the ceiling details as well as the rest of the surroundings. Quite satisfactory for a limited shot, this technique is restrictive, and requires correct camera positioning to be effective.

For palatial interiors, perspective ceiling treatment has been introduced by a scenic cloth hung behind the low flattage of a built set. Then, in long shots, the ceiling cloth is seen combined with the setting. But again, camera positions are quite restricted for effective results, as scenic perspective has necessarily to relate to a particular viewpoint.

This difficulty can be circumvented, of course, by using a plain background or cyc cloth to suggest the ceiling. Provided the director does not shoot high up the cloth, and force all lighting units to be rigged higher up to keep them out of shot (thereby creating steep lighting angles), this subterfuge can be remarkably convincing. It may not be practicable, though, to light the ceiling cloth with appropriate intensity or evenness, especially where it is curved or shaped.

Mattes

Camera matte. Although the camera matte is again only suitable for a single fixed camera set-up, it can, if properly prepared, offer quite elaborate illusions. A vertical cut-out representing a ceiling is set up in the top area of a camera's field of view. The camera shoots the studio scene through this cut-out (a considerable depth of field is necessary), and the foreground matte and staging blend into a combined picture. Simple enough in principle, there may be incompatible perspective, incorrect scale or tonal balance, or the edges of the matte may be too defocused to register with the built set. However, as a glass shot (with the matte painted instead on a vertical glass panel) this method has formed the foundation for many motion picture scenic effects.

Electronic matte. Here, a picture of a ceiling piece is inserted electronically into the picture of the studio scene (page 154). Now certain problems of the camera matte method are overcome, for depth of field is no longer so critical and the masked area combines with a hard edge to the framing the camera makes of the setting. However, because the camera itself is, in fact, shooting over the studio set—to introduce space in its shot for the ceiling to appear in—precautions should be taken to prevent it from seeing bright lamps hung above the staging. Unlike the camera matte, which masks them off, they are clearly visible to the studio camera during electronic matting, and may leave damaging 'burns' on the camera tube.

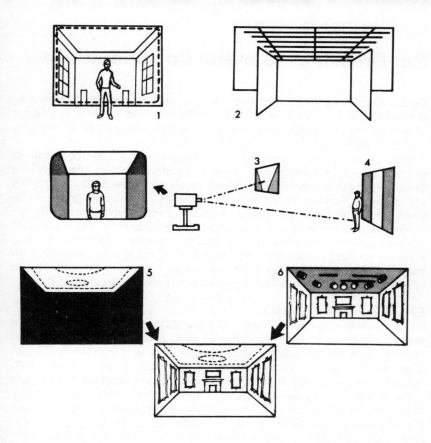

CEILINGS – SUBSTITUTION METHODS

Background cloth

1, Total detail of the ceiling and the environment can be included on a scenic background – painted or photographic ; 2, A cloth can be hung behind low scenery, to be seen as a ceiling when the camera shoots over. The cloth may be plain (e.g. a cyc-cloth), or painted in perspective.

Foreground camera matte

The camera sees both the matte in the foreground, 3, and the background scene 4.

Electronic matte

A picture of a ceiling, 5, e.g. a graphic – is inserted into the corresponding portion of a shot, 6. The top of the shot is blanked out electronically, and the matte is seen in its place.

Set Dressing—General Considerations

Fundamentally, *set dressing* involves the choice and arrangement of the multitude of items that 'clothe' the bare scenic staging. The range of articles required will clearly vary with the type and style of production, and selections made by any individual designer.

With the most basic treatment, a discussion programme could consist of two people standing and talking together. But notice how the character of the presentation changes subtly as we gradually add to the set dressing: chairs (upright or armchairs?), a central table, water carafe, drinking glasses, ashtrays, a carpet, background drapes, etc.

Set dressing is a very personal art. It may be carried out by a separate specialist, or by the set designer and his assistant. Dressing staging involves so much more than selecting and hiring appropriate props for the occasion, and locating these rationally. It means engendering the very essence of a scene; characteristics that create individuality.

Effectiveness on camera

When choosing set dressings, the wily designer thinks not only of their environmental suitability, but of their probable effectiveness on camera, and the technical idiosyncracies of the TV system. Certain materials in furnishings and drapes can introduce difficulties. Deep velvets and velours tend to look 'dead' and unmodelled. White lace curtains must be *dipped* (dyed) to a light coffee-colour, grey or blue, to prevent their 'burning out' distractingly on camera. Plastic, plasticised, glazed materials and generally shiny articles are liable to cause troublesome flares. Where the required item is a technical hazard, one can only use it, and hope that any 'doctoring' (dulling spray, spraying down, or similar treatment) will alleviate problems.

The televised scene soon acquires a filled-up look. Simplicity is often the keynote of success. Careful selection and positioning is preferable to abundance and, certainly, too much dressing is uneconomic, distracting, confusing. Remember, it is what the camera sees and registers clearly that counts. It is all too easy to assume that certain favourite period props add realism to a scene, when in fact they are virtually unnoticed by the viewer.

Detached appraisal

Working in the studio, the greatest difficulty is to stand back and appraise the situation as the viewer will be doing, seeing it for the first and only time. First impressions are hard to anticipate. Particularly after working hard on a project, we are inclined to excuse or justify its shortcomings, or to overrate the impact of aspects that have taken time and trouble to arrange, or forget that the viewer never has free visual selection, but sees only what the camera reveals. These are the intrinsic truths of all presentational media.

SET DRESSINGS – GENERAL CONSIDERATIONS

Initial stages

One starts with the bare skeleton of the set – architecturally appropriate for the situation.

It is now personalised, in a fashion suitable for the period, the people and the action. Carefully selected properties will enhance the scene, give it conviction, yet do not cause it to look over-fussy, clog composition, or impede the camera. An over-dressed or ineffectively dressed set does not have additional 'character'. It just becomes confused and unattractive. Occasionally this may be exactly the effect we want to convey.

It is one thing to look at furniture, but quite another to use it!

Set Dressings—Furniture

Apart from the more obvious needs to choose furniture of appropriate style, period, and so on, there are several very practical matters that we should not overlook when appraising furnishings for a production.

Practical hazards

If there are seats for interviews, are they comfortable enough, or will the people be tempted to fidget and wriggle in an attempt to sit at ease?

Does the chair suit the performer? One sees big, bulky men perched on light framed chairs, and small women lost in large armchairs.

Is the chair static, or can it be turned and so enable the performer to reposition himself? Swivel seats or armchairs that travel as one sits in them are troublesome. Frontal shots that the director has carefully lined up, can be aborted as the subject twists himself into a profile position.

Low seats in armchairs or settees are often frustratingly difficult to get into gracefully, cause ungainly seated posture, encourage lounging, and are tiresome to get out of. All these points work against the general aim of smooth camera treatment and presentation. Extra cushions may help to build up the seat and back to improve matters.

Try to avoid armchairs with wings or head supports that shield off the face in profile.

Beware of wickerwork seats and any other creaking furniture. Rocking chairs, too, can be fun to ride back and forth in, but are a nuisance to shoot.

These noises all too easily become intrusive when picked up by the microphone and exaggerated.

Taming the unruly

Polished table-tops by their nature tend to reflect back-light straight into the camera lens. Shiny surfaces may be dulled down with wax spray, to improve matters, or obscured with a suitably toned material (e.g. a table cover). For certain situations, it may be best to break up large bare areas on foreground tables (or desks), dressing them with appropriate props—table mats, blotter pad, books, flowers, etc.

If orthodox furniture proves to be too low for comfort or to suit the shot, it may be *blocked up*, either completely on scenic blocks, or under each leg with wooden furniture blocks (about 4 in high, square or cylindrical and recessed at one end). Strange looking, perhaps, if inadvertently seen on camera, the blocks will often be masked by other furniture, or very occasionally they can be disguised with cloth or paper gaiters. Don't try moving such furniture during a performance!

Items can be accented or subdued by deliberately controlling their colour and brightness relative to nearby subjects and backgrounds. The contrast of light on dark, or dark on light, will give prominence and emphasis. Fairly similar toned surfaces may merge completely!

SET DRESSING – FURNITURE

Seating one comes to know!
1, The swivel chair effect ; 2, The low recliner ; 3, The precarious perch ;
4, The hard surface ; 5, The mobile armchair ; 6, The intimacy of wing
armchairs.

Remedies for unsuitable furniture
7, Where a person's position does not suit the camera, cushions can be added to
adjust posture, and bring him to a convenient height. 8, Where furniture is not at
a height suitable for good composition, it can be blocked up.

Set Dressing—Practical Lamps

In TV staging, a considerable variety of low-wattage light fittings are used to furnish settings. Most of these are familiar domestic fittings, and include wall-lamps, table and stand lamps, chandeliers, etc.

Apart from the necessary, but easily overlooked, precaution of ensuring that the fittings are electrically safe, care must be taken with their trailing leads. These are best taped to the studio floor. Cables for wall lamps can usually be concealed by running them through a small hole in the flat behind the bracket. The fitting itself may be screwed to the flat, or hung from a metal S or Z hook in a corresponding hole.

To be effective, a practical lamp should not only appear to be alight, but should seem to be illuminating the nearby setting and people appropriately. This may seem obvious enough, but is not always readily accomplished under studio conditions. Most practical lamps are of relatively low power, and provide insufficient illumination for their surroundings when matched with the intense studio lighting the TV camera needs. High power bulbs such as photofloods can be introduced into some fittings but can overheat the unit when burned for some time. Ironically, the normal light-pattern and quality from the fitting will generally have to be simulated by studio lighting.

Practical problems
In choosing practical lighting fittings, certain design features are worth bearing in mind. Bare-bulb fittings can prove over-bright on camera, and cause video defects such as streaking or lag effects. Dimmed to give no trouble, their lamps can look strangely unconvincing. Lampshades, too, have their complications. Dark shades may look unlit from some angles, due to their density, while from others, their reflective white linings can easily be over-bright for the camera. Light-toned shades, white opal globes, and similar fittings continue to appear bright, even when unlit, as they catch general lighting around the set.

Controlling practicals
Practical lamps of adjustable intensity such as oil lamps and hurricane lanterns can pose problems for the video engineer if they burn too brightly. Battery-powered substitutes are of constant brightness, but generally less realistic. If a candle is too bright, trim its wick.

Gas fittings of all types are best adjusted remotely for suitable flow, so that the appliance itself can be turned on fully by a performer. This method ensures more predictable results. Where a gas supply is not available or convenient, a wall fitting made be made electrical. A suitably shaped frosted pygmy lamp (15 watts) may substitute for the gas mantle. Even an inoperable street lamp has been made to appear working by illuminating it with a localised spotlight.

Lamps

Practical lamps take a wide variety of
forms ; Many are the familiar, domestic-
type electrical fittings.

Substitutes

Practical electric devices can also
simulate oil or gas-burning fittings. An
electric lamp operating from an internal
battery or a mains supply, replaces the
original light source.

Decorative light can be like jewels, rich and enhancing, or tawdry and distracting.

Set Dressing—Decorative Light Fittings

Illuminated fittings add realism to an exterior night scene, with advertisements, traffic-signs, street lamps.

There are three methods of achieving such effects: Direct, indirect, and simulated approaches.

In the *direct* approach, we use the real thing; actual signs, illuminated globes, a string of bare light bulbs. However, do not underestimate the problems in making up, transporting, installing, and powering these fittings. Careful grounding/earthing is essential. Bare lamps are very vulnerable.

Sometimes a complete effect can be convincingly achieved by *indirect* means instead. For example, a single lamp in a light-box with a painted translucent panel, can imitate an elaborate multiple display, or a 'neon sign'.

An even more economical substitute is the *simulated effect*. Here a black 'non-reflective' surface (e.g. flock-paper) has highly reflective designs stuck on it; using lettering cut out in metal foil, plastic sheet, reflex screen material, even white paper, which appears lit up when illuminated by a strong spotlight.

Opportunities . . . and warnings

Reliability and safety are important factors for all decorative fittings. Impromptu lash-ups can result not only in odd individual lights in a total effect going 'on the blink', but where a random lamp fails in a continuous arrangement, the gappy disruption can prove quite distracting.

Particularly where strings of bulbs are used (such as around rostra edges, on cut-outs, in hung festoons) they should be properly supported and held away from all scenery and drapes.

Pea-lamps/Christmas tree lights

Small pea-lamps, flash-lamp bulbs, Christmas tree lights, can usefully imitate distant light sources. By pinning them to a black cyc cloth, we can simulate street lamps, harbour lights, runway indicators, stars.

Flashing lights

Lamps can be switched rhythmically or intermittently. They can be flashed in time with the programme audio. They can be arranged as 'chaser lights', in which rapid successive switching creates the impression of light movement.

Switching can be mechanical (by hand, or thermo-couple) or by automatic circuits (controlled by cassettes; computer programmed). Notwithstanding the added realism or the excitement of rhythmically flashing lights, we must always consider whether a spectacular effect is likely to become fidgety or distracting.

SET DRESSING – DECORATIVE LIGHT FITTINGS

Illuminated signs
Street, advertising, and locational signs add realism.

Decorative light effects
Decorative light effects can be introduced in staging by methods including
1, Decorative cyclorama lighting ; 2, Hanging festoons of lamps ; 3, Skeletal
framework structures of lamps ; 4, Edge lamps, which are normal low-wattage
bulbs in batten-fitted holders ; 5, Glitter-faced panels reflecting localised
spotlights. Facing materials include glass chips, sequins, mica flakes, reflective
plastic flake ; 6, Internally illuminated stairway and rostra, e.g. plastic-faced
plate glass panels ; 7, Illuminated panels by hidden strip-lights ; 8, Tinsel
curtains consisting of thin silver plastic foil strips.

At its best, greenery gives exteriors absolute conviction. At its worst, the effect is pathetic.

Set Dressing—Greenery

The hot lights of TV studios are unkind to most flowers and foliage, and colours become exaggerated by the camera. So the best effect is not always achieved by the most obvious approach.

TV staging uses three categories of 'greenery':

1. *Living greenery*—potted plants, shrubs, turf, etc.
2. *Dead greenery*—tree branches, felled saplings, grass tussocks, rushes, ivy, autumn leaves, etc.
3. *Artificial* greenery—plastic flowers and foliage, grass matting, etc.

Living greenery

Living greenery needs periodic water-spraying to keep it fresh. Try to keep cut flowers out of lights as long as possible.

Turf can be conjoined to form convincing sward, but soon becomes trampled if walked on. Tall grasses and bamboo clumps provide effective greenery, where appropriate, to a studio 'exterior'.

Potted shrubs create 'authentic' undergrowth, their tubs being hidden by tufts of coarse grass, by peat or sawdust mounds, or grass matting.

Dead greenery

Tree branches may remain sufficiently fresh-looking for the programme duration, but, with time, leaves curl and the withered result can only be used realistically in distant staging areas. Tree branches or saplings can be held upright by timber bracing or by tubular metal *tree stands* held stable with concealed stage weights. Leafless trees and branches provide winter tracery and store effectively. Sprayed white or silver, they have decorative applications.

Materials including ivy, creeper and evergreen foliage, have wide uses as set dressings.

Artificial greenery

Plastic flowers can be used in floral arrangements, 'planted' in garden beds, attached to other greenery as 'blossom', stapled as 'climbing plants' on walls, etc.

Tree trunks are convincingly constructed from moulded glass fibre or rubber assemblies (on a timber framework), augmented by real tree branches stuck into strategic holes.

Hedges can be made by fixing foliage (e.g. box or cypress) to an expanded metal frame, or into a timber base. The lightweight result is conveniently mobile if fitted with wheels.

Grass represented by raffia or plastic matting is more believable if cropped locally to give an uneven 'growth height', and sprayed to give variations of colour and tone.

Peat sprinkled here and there is an invaluable standby to help break-up any over-formality of either natural or artificial greenery arrangements.

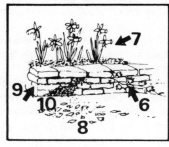

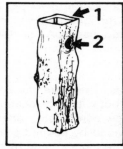

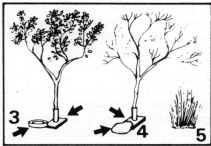

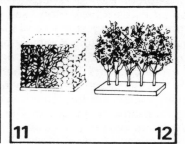

SET DRESSING – GREENERY

Living greenery
Where greenery is to be handled or seen closely, only living foliage is generally convincing.

Tree trunk
1, Rubber or glass fibre tree trunk on timber frame ; 2, Hole provided for insertion of natural tree branch.

Natural 'dead' greenery
3, Natural leafy branch in weighted tree stand ; 4, Decorative, whitened branch ; 5, Dried grass tussock.

Typical 'plastic gardening'
6, Creeper ; 7, plastic flowers in peat ; 8, leaves dried or plastic ; 9, glass fibre 'stone walling' ; 10, ivy real or plastic.

Hedges
Artificial hedge constructed from : 11, cypress branches on wire-net frame, or 12, vertical tree branches in a wooden board.

Effective backings can turn a 'set' into a 'location'.

Backings

As we saw earlier (page 92), *backings* prevent the camera from inadvertently shooting outside the confines of the scene. But backings represent much more than just masking surfaces. They augment the setting, provide continuation and extend the viewers' impressions of the total environment.

Beyond an arch, a glazed partition, or an open door, we see aspects of adjoining rooms and corridors. We discover architectural relationships. Outside a window, we perceive signs of the building's locality. We have indications of the weather, the time of day, the season, perhaps. The external elements can impinge upon our room; sunlight casts shadows on the walls, or rain may beat against the window panes. An enclosed room tells us none of these things.

Forms of backing

In practice, backings take several regular forms. There are the *basic backings*, simply denoting further scenic planes, but with little locational association—flattage (plain, papered or surface contoured), drapes, cycloramas. *Flat pictorial backings* can be provided by painted scenic cloths, by photographic 'blow-ups' (P.B.U., photo murals), and by rear projection (B.P., back projection—see page 152). *Built extensions* may be constructed to suggest the continuation of staging, from the juxtaposition of a few flats, to completely built locational areas, for example showing all the salient features of an adjoining room. *Electronically inserted backings* (page 154) too, can be effectively used.

For the overall effect to be convincing, pictorial backings should substantially match the foreground scene—in proportion, perspective, colour-relationships, lighting, etc. The eye-level of foreground camera and background picture should also match, or the result will give an incongruous uphill or downhill illusion. It may be necessary to raise or lower the backing to achieve balanced eye-levels and also avoid spurious shadows spilling over pictorial backing, destroying its realism.

Obscured openings

There are circumstances in which no space is available to set up backings, or none is wanted. For these, the opening may be closed off with drapes, blinds, shutters, etc. A window can be blanked-off with translucent materials such as gauzes (page 124), light drapes (ninons, sheers, lace curtains), frosted or obscured plastic sheeting, ornamental glass substitutes (in ribbed, hammered or moulded formations). Where the situation allows, such blind translucent surfaces can have environmental shadows cast onto them from their reverse side. Leaf shadows suggest nearby foliage, window-bar shadows imply confinement etc.

Backing effectiveness

1, Rear wall window backing clearly
visible on frontal cameras 2, and both
cross shooting cameras, 3 and 4 ; A
side wall window backing 5, is unseen
by Camera 3, and is most evident on
Camera 4. Hence backing 1, has good
continual locational association, while
backing 5 has much less.

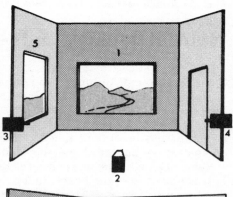

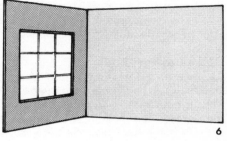

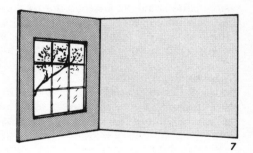

The value of backings

6, A blank window tells nothing of
environment or location. It can only
imply 'day' or 'night' ; 7, An obscured
(e.g. frosted) window where a tree
branch shadow suggests sunlight and
the tree shows that it is not winter ; 8,
A scenic backing reveals the location of
the scene. Sunlight entering suggests
possible weather, time of day, etc.

109

Neutral Backgrounds—Plain

Plain backgrounds of tones that contrast with the subject, can provide visual *isolation*, making the subject stand out from its surroundings. The closer the subject tones to those of the background, the more they will tend to merge. Dark clothing against dark tones in walls, furniture, foliage, or light-toned clothing against pale scenic tones are an anathema—but they happen, nevertheless.

Remember, too, that one can easily be fooled by *colour differentiation.* The fact that subject and background have differing hues does not mean that the relative tones will be distinctly different in a monochrome picture. They could reproduce as similar shades of grey. Nor must the need for effective visual impact in the black and white picture be overlooked.

Black backgrounds
An overall *black background* (page 4) has its staging drawbacks. Dark hair has been known to merge with it, to produce 'instant baldness'. Strong backlight overcomes this problem, and models the hair—but in the process can make it appear over-shiny or frizzy.

Plain black backgrounds are easy to achieve. A run of black cotton drapes, a black floor (painted or covered) and any dark areas that remain visible can usually be *crushed out* by the video operator's adjustment of the camera channel's *black level* (the video being *sat, set-down, batting down on blacks*). But if there is too much video adjustment there is a progressive loss of gradation in other darker tones also.

Light backgrounds
Plain light backgrounds are provided by a white cyclorama—actually off-white, with a maximum reflectance of around 70%. White materials are generally more critical, in that creases, folds, dirtying, tears, etc., are plainly visible whereas black materials can become comparatively neglected and not show it. One can blank-out white areas electronically, within limits by increased lighting intensity, white clipping or *crushing out* the video to an even, overall white tone. But care must be taken not to destroy modelling of lighter tones in other subjects.

Cycloramas have the advantage over extended flattage, that there are no joins to disrupt the smooth surface. Conversely, they require careful hanging and stretching to achieve a smooth plane.

Mid-tone backgrounds
Mid-grey backgrounds have to be chosen and lit with care, for their values can come perilously near to that of many face tones. Skin reflectance is typically about 30-40% (TV white is 70%; TV black is $3\frac{1}{2}$%). Careful lighting can, over wide limits, lighten or darken backgrounds to improve the subject-to-background contrast.

NEUTRAL BACKGROUNDS –
PLAIN BACKGROUNDS

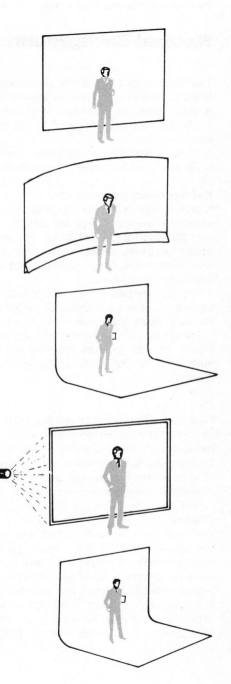

Single plain flat
This provides a plain background but is only suitable for relatively close shots. Joins between flats must be carefully obscured (page 52) and edge lighting avoided.

Cyclorama
This offers an unbroken background over a wide angle. Floor tone may be made similar to cyc, and a cove used to merge the planes.

Seamless background
A seamless background avoids any background/floor join, but the width limits camera mobility, and draped cloth is not readily stretched taut to reduce wrinkles.

Translucent screen
The screen can be rear-lit to required brightness, but even overall illumination is difficult to obtain.

Chroma key background
Here the picture's chroma-key background (e.g. blue) is electronically replaced by any chosen hue or tone from another source.

Neutral Backgrounds—Non-Associative

The purist might argue that no background can be truly non-associative. Most stimuli tend to promote associated ideas. Even the plainest background tones are reminiscent of certain moods and conditions:
1. White: delicacy, simplicity, lightness, cheerfulness, sparkle, vigour, snow . . .
2. Grey: depression, inactivity, calmness, decay . . .
3. Black: night, mystery, heaviness, sombreness, smartness . . .

Background pattern
Nevertheless, it is possible to devise backgrounds that provide pleasing, attractive surroundings for action, and yet will not have conscious associations for the audience. For example, an indefinite, vague pattern of light shapes and shadows can be used to effectively break up an otherwise bare, blank background without creating environmental or emotional overtones.

But if that pattern is focused to make it distinct, and clear-cut, it begins to take on individual pictorial significance. We now find ourselves reacting to the line, shape, mass and tonal distribution we see.

For the set designer, this change is more than an interesting academic nicety. He appreciates that the potential impact staging has upon an audience can be altered according to its prominence, contrast and clarity.

Contrast
One can emphasise or subdue staging by choice of tone and hue, by firmness of line. Harsh, hard, clear-cut contrasting staging, or scenic backgrounds painted softly on black gauze, worked in diffused air-brush techniques, have all been explored successfully to control this relationship between the subject and its surroundings, and the strength of the background's associative influence.

Clarity
The *lens aperture or f stop* on the camera will also affect the clarity of the scene. Using a large lens aperture (shallow depth of field), the subject tends to be isolated and background detail blurred. But if the same lens is stopped down (i.e. a smaller lens aperture is used, so giving a greater depth of field) the shot becomes more sharply-focused overall, showing distinct detail in both subject and surroundings. So we can influence the overall clarity of the staging by adjusting the lens aperture, and/or by balancing relative light intensities.

NEUTRAL BACKGROUNDS – NON-ASSOCIATIVE BACKGROUNDS

Shadow clarity

1, Strong shadow patterns on the background tend to become associative. Their shape influences pictorial composition.

2, Defocused shadows tend to become unassociated and vague, and yet attractively disrupt what would otherwise be a blank-looking background.

Varying background clarity

Backgrounds tend to become less associative as camera shots get closer. Firstly, less staging can be seen as shots 'tighten'. Secondly, the available depth of field decreases progressively. At larger lens apertures (such as f1.9) this depth becomes further reduced.

Background Lighting—Shading

The evenness with which we light a scenic plane can have a considerable influence on its appearance, and upon our interpretation of the picture.

Even lighting

Certain types of background require flat, even lighting if they are to appear convincing. For example, a photo-enlargement providing an 'exterior scene', backing outside the window of an apartment will normally be lit to a similar intensity overall to achieve a realistic effect.

Generally speaking, we shall find that if we light scenic planes flatly, they tend to take on an open-air look, a vastness, emptiness and plainness. These qualities may be quite appropriate. To suggest the infinite, overall even lighting on an expanse of white cyclorama would be ideal.

If, on the other hand, we were to light the walls of a room similarly, with flat, unbroken light, the result would be unsatisfying. The interior would look baldly artificial. It might even cease to look like an interior at all !

Temporal shading

Although variations of light and shade in a scene create visual interest, they need to be meaningful and systematic, suiting the particular situation.

The way light falls within a room, often becomes associated with certain times of day. During daylight, for instance, the window wall of a room will be darker than others, with the level of illumination falling off according to the distance a surface is from it. At night, the relative brightnesses and positions of the light fittings within the room determine the distribution of light and shade. When a room has dark-toned walls (e.g. dingy panelling) it can be quite difficult to achieve a convincing daylight effect, if no window is visible.

Spatial shading

Vertical background shading influences our impressions of the apparent height and size of an interior. As shading is moved downwards so that a greater area of the upper wall is unlit, or in relative shadow, the room feels progressively smaller, and the ceiling lower (even if there isn't one !). Thus, a lofty palace scene would usually have its walls shaded higher than a claustrophobic cottage interior.

Even where backgrounds are purely decorative or abstract, the influence of wall shading persists, and modifies the staging impact.

Graded background tones have the very practical properties, too, of enabling us to alter the prominence of various parts of the scene—throwing some areas into sharper relief and making others less conspicuous. Likewise, wall shading can be introduced to emphasise the outlines of people, scenic units or furniture.

Background shading

As the background is progressively shaded, the picture develops a more 'closed-in' feel. The subject tends to become more prominent. 1, This open-air effect, if applied to interior-type staging, creates an artificial, unconvincing atmosphere. 2, Typical shading for a lofty interior lit by daylight. 3, Shading for a daylit interior scene with a 'normal' ceiling height (e.g. 8–10 ft.) 4, Shading for evening interior scene, or more dramatic daytime interiors. 5, A strongly-shaded wall creates a confined, restricted, or nocturnal effect. It can be applied successfully to low-ceilinged rooms, boat and aircraft interiors etc.

Pattern treatments with light are limited only by the imagination (and facilities, and time . . .)

Background Lighting — Patterns

As we discussed on page 112, the clarity of light patterns can be adjusted from an indecipherable blur, to sharp, strong, clear-cut shapes that appear as if painted on the background. Light and pigment are often so similar in their effect, that we can use one or the other equally well to give the illusion of contour or to introduce surface patterns.

In broad terms, patterns can be created by lighting in three ways:
1. Cast shadow—Here a light beam is interrupted by an opaque body such as a window, foliage, decorative cut-out or stencil.
2. Projected shadow—A projector focuses the image of a photo-slide, metal sheet, or foil stencil onto the background.
3. Silhouetted shadow—The subject is unlit against a light background, or its shadow cast from the rear onto a translucent background.

If we use luminants of differing hues, their shadows and half-shadows will become multi-coloured from the lights and their mixtures.

Practical problems

There are inherent problems in the use of light patterns where we need sharp, contrasty, or accurately delineated shapes (e.g. lettering, or geometrical patterns).
1. Stability—The patterns should be held firmly in position.
2. Dilution—Spill-light from other lamps or reflected from nearby surfaces, can dilute and pale-out shadows.
3. Sharpness—The sharpness of *cast shadows* and silhouettes is greatest when point light sources are used. (Their light rays are virtually parallel.) Sharpness is greatest, too, when the shadowing object is relatively close to the background, and the light source distant.

Projected shadows rely on a focused optical system for their sharpness. Where the stencil has depth (i.e. is multi-layer, or not entirely flat), or the background itself is sloping or curved relative to the projector axis, the image will not be sharp overall.
4. Size—The size of cast shadow increases with the distance of the shadowing object from the background, and with the closeness of the lamp to the object.

When a projector is used, the image size increases with its distance (*throw*) and its lens angle is widened (i.e. its focal length shortened).
5. Distortion—Only when lamps or projectors are at right angles to a surface will shadows be *un*distorted.

Light pattern opportunities are legion: lettering (locational, identifying); stylised patterns of flowers, designs, architectural features; realistic effects (foliage shadows, light from leaded windows, prison bars); abstract effects (reflected patterns, defocused or diffuse shapes); colour patterns (single or multi-hue, blends, associative hues).

Moving light patterns may be created by motorised projectors, mirror-balls, metal foil reflections or rotating cut-outs.

BACKGROUND LIGHTING TREATMENT – PATTERNS

Lighting patterns

1, With a 'cast shadow' a frame or cut-out placed in the light beam casts a shadow ; 2, With a 'projected shadow' a projector throws the image of a photo-slide or metal stencil on to a background ; 3, With a silhouetted shadow the subject is unlit against a brighter background, which is illuminated from the front or from behind a translucent background.

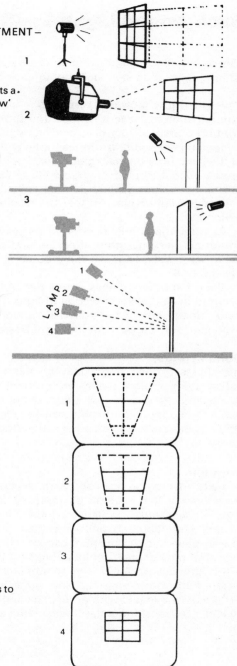

Shadow distortion

Only when the lamp is at right angles to the shadowing object and to the background plane, will the resulting shadow be undistorted. The more oblique the shadow projection, the greater will be the distortion. Overall sharpness will deteriorate also.

Light coverage can be controlled by quite simple devices.

Background Lighting—Shapes

Simple but effective light variations are possible on a background, using nothing more than standard spotlights and *barndoor* accessories.

The spotlight's characteristics
Pointed straight-on to a surface, the spotlight provides a round disc of light. The area of this disc can be adjusted within limits by *flooding* (spreading) or *spotting* (concentrating) the light beam. As the distance of the lamp from the background is increased, the size of the spot or disc grows. Some *spotlights* (*luminaires, lanterns*) produce hard-edged beams with sharp clearly defined limits, but most TV spotlights have soft-edged light beams so that the resultant light shape has a diffused periphery.

As the lamp is fully flooded to cover its maximum area, its attached barndoors become more effective, and enable us to cut off the light beam selectively. Thus we can produce slits or rectangles of light on the background.

When a spotlight shines onto a flat surface from an oblique angle, its beam forms a divergent wedge of light. This may be firmly defined, if a hard-edged spot or large-area barndoors are used, while for an un-restricted, soft-edged spot, the light beam has diffuse edges.

Gobos (flags)
Flat sheets (*gobos, flags*) may be hung a few feet in front of spot-lights to cut off light beams with a hard or soft edge. If this surface is stencilled (e.g. with a new moon, rising sun, or similar form) a definite pattern of light of controllable size and clarity may be cast. Less identifiable cut out stencil shapes (or silhouettes) will produce more abstract forms.

Dappling
A multi-opening stencil can create several light shapes from the same lamp beam. The extreme example of this is the *cookie* (cucoloris, dapple sheet, cuke) which produces effects ranging from a subtle or pronounced dapple to sinuous veining, according to its design. Pieces of transparent colour medium can be introduced into the various openings, and provide multi-coloured light shapes on the background.

A further development is an area of colour medium, supported a short distance in front of a lamp, and stencilled (effective for vague cloud patterns), or overlaid with other pieces of colour medium. The resultant shapes can transform a flat undecorated surface.

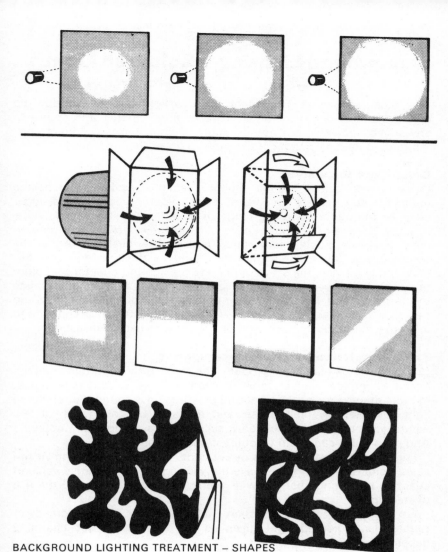

BACKGROUND LIGHTING TREATMENT – SHAPES

Spotlight
As a spotlight is 'flooded', it covers a larger area, its light intensity diminishes and shadows become sharper.

Barndoor
Hinged barndoor flaps may be used singly, in pairs, or in combinations to produce strips, squares and rectangles of light of adjustable size. The fitting rotates to place the large or small barndoor flap assembly at any angle between the vertical and the horizontal.

Cookie (cucoloris or cuke)
A metal stencil is placed in front of a spotlight to produce shadows, ranging from subtle dappling to strong blotches and light patterns.

119

Coloured light offers many opportunities, but also many traps for the unwary.

Background Lighting—Coloured Light

In a 'black and white' TV system coloured light can only modify the grey scale rendering of coloured surfaces it illuminates, and appeal to any studio audience, but nothing more. Colour makes no direct contribution to the final impact of the show in these circumstances.

Colour and the viewer

Working with colour TV, the situation remains similar as far as the monochrome viewer is concerned. If the coloured cyc behind a singer changes through a beguiling range of hues, on the 'black and white' receiver, it remains a singer and a varying grey background, nothing more. However much colour appeal is used, we must ensure that the compatible version of the picture still maintains effective tonal contrast.

With this proviso, the set designer and the lighting director for colour television have every opportunity to express ideas that are appropriate to the production through the use of colour. Colour gives vitality and personality to staging. Coloured lighting can attract attention and influence mood. But if used wrongly, the results can be disastrous.

The appropriateness of coloured lighting

Coloured illumination can produce the most bizarre portrait lighting. Coloured light can, in fact, rarely be used on faces for serious purposes. In most drama productions, lighting directors have found that coloured light has relatively limited use, and tends to be confined to a few naturalistic or stylised effects only, such as skies, firelight or moonlight. And even these can strain credulity if mishandled.

For straight shows, such as discussions, demonstrations and newscasts, coloured lighting may have the very practical decorative value of enabling us to ring changes with scenic hues, and so extend the use of staging.

For 'display' types of production, including music, dance, comedy or spectacular, coloured light gives us the opportunity for changing decorative effects.

Although, on the face of it, we would seem to have the full spectrum from which to choose for staging, it is both intriguing and frustrating in practice to discover that only a rather small range can be used unobtrusively and tastefully. Our subjective impression of flesh tones can be considerably modified by the background colour against which we see them. Because faces tend to take on the complementary hue of their surroundings, they can accordingly appear pallid, ruddy, greenish or even bluish. This rather limits the possible selection for normal purposes. Certain pale blue, straw, pink, amber and lavender tints have proved very suitable, while backgrounds lit with red, green, yellow, purple or violet, generally become too vibrant, overpowering, or distracting for more serious applications where close range portraiture is involved.

120

BACKGROUND LIGHTING TREATMENT –
COLOURED LIGHT

Light mixture

Coloured light mixes in an additive
manner. It's primaries are red, green,
and blue light. A mixture of red and
green light produces yellow light.
Red and blue light together produces
magenta light. Green and blue
light mix to produce cyan (blue-
green) light. Red, green and blue
light mix to give 'white' light. Black
is an absence of reflected light.

Surface colours

When light falls on a surface, some
is absorbed, some reflected. White
light contains the entire continuous
spectral range of colours intermixed.
(Red, orange, yellow, green, blue,
indigo, violet.) If passed through a
prism, these component hues are
separately distinguishable. As light
illuminates a surface, its component
hues are absorbed in various
proportions. The resulting effect, we
call the colour of that surface. Thus,
a 'white' surface reflects all spectral
hues to some degree. A red surface
mostly reflects red light, absorbing
other hues. A black surface absorbs
all hues, reflecting little of any.

Coloured light on coloured
surfaces

1. Where coloured light falls on a
white or grey surface, the area will
appear as a shade of that colour ; 2,
If it falls on a surface of impure
colour (most reflect a range of hues),
some light of its own hue will be
reflected ; 3, When coloured light
falls on a surface reflecting *none* of
its own hue (e.g. red light onto a
green area) the surface appears
black. In monochrome TV these
effects can be used to alter
reproduced surface tone (Samoiloff
effect).

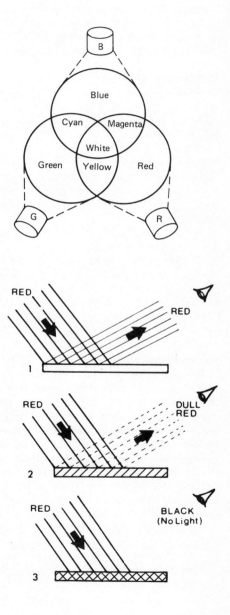

121

Translucent Backgrounds

Translucent backgrounds provide an extremely useful range of staging opportunities for the designer. In a small studio, they can be introduced as a general utility background, which may be quickly modified to suit the requirements of a particular production (page 80).

Suitable materials
Various materials can be used to construct the translucent background, including stretched cloth and plastic sheeting. Off-white or light grey surfaces are preferable, with a matte finish to reduce reflections from studio lighting.

A range of uses
We can use these translucent backgrounds in various ways:
1. As a plain background of adjustable brightness and hue. Remember, though, any joins, supports or stretchers will show through when lit from the rear.
2. As a shaded background, lit from below with strip lights (ground row, floor trough, cyc lights).
3. For displaying light patterns and shapes.
4. Decorated by silhouetted ornamental screens, foliage, etc., located behind it.
5. To display projected pictures.
6. As lit translucent panelling to back display shelves, skeletal scenery, etc.

Frontal lighting
Although any frontal spill light will necessarily dilute the density of shadows cast upon their surfaces, translucent backgrounds have the dual advantage of versatility, and of allowing treatment to be altered instantly by lighting or scenic rearrangement. Frontal lighting or front projection from the camera side of the screen may be used to supplement or replace rear lighting, and so provide a further series of displays—perhaps while rear-projected effects are being changed.

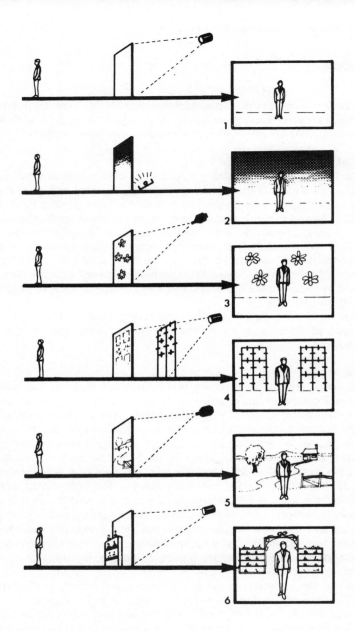

TRANSLUCENT BACKGROUNDS

Background versatility

The translucent background has versatility. It can be used 1, as a plain background ; 2, as a shaded background ; 3, for displaying light-patterns and shapes ; 4, for ornamental silhouettes ; 5, for projected pictures ; 6, as a lit background for silhouetted scenery, (skeletal, cut-outs), shelf-units, etc.

Gauzes

Gauze (*scrim*) is one of the staple staging materials, for it can be used and re-used in many interesting ways. It can, in fact, provide a variety of scenic effects that are not readily achieved by any other means.

Forms of gauzes

Gauze is basically a thin netting (usually of cotton) of around $\frac{1}{16}$ in to $\frac{1}{8}$ in (1·5 to 3 mm) diameter. Available in black, grey or white, it can be sprayed or dipped if necessary, to different shades of colours. It can be hung in drape form, but is usually stretched in most applications.

Stock gauzes. These are large-area gauzes (e.g. over 15 ft high and 30 ft long), which stretched over cyclorama cloths to obscure any irregularities in the surface of the cyc, and to assist in creating an illusion of infinite space before the camera. Wrinkles and creases are eliminated by securing the top edge, and weighting the lower edge under battens or tubular bars.

Sometimes the stretched gauze is pitched (sloped) at an angle to enable ground-lighting to be positioned between the gauze and the cyclorama.

Applications

Atmospheric effects. Gauze facing-techniques are also used to soften-off the artificiality of artist-painted or photographic pictorial back-grounds. The result is an 'atmospheric haze', only otherwise obtained by a light spattering of white or grey paint, or delicate air-brush work.

Scenic gauze. When the camera shoots a subject located behind a stretched gauze, certain intriguing lighting effects become possible. Lit from the camera side only, the gauze surface looks solid and the far subject is unseen—provided no light passes through the gauze to reveal it. If the subject is now illuminated it appears, with detail softened by the gauze, which is still visible, particularly if surface painted. If only the subject area is lit and the gauze itself left unlit, it virtually disappears, except for the silhouettes of any surface detail or painting that may be on it. Scenic gauzes are particularly useful, therefore, for transformations and mysterious effects.

Gauze has been painted to simulate scenery, realistically or in abstract form, with economy and delicacy not provided in built staging.

Glass substitute. Gauze may be used as a non-reflective substitute in shop windows, supporting lettering or motifs. Pieces of gauze can be stapled to the windows or studio interior scenes to reduce the clarity or sharpness of scenery outside. On location, localised gauze may help to hold back the prominence of exterior views, reducing their brightness.

Contrast control. Black gauze can sometimes lower the contrast of scenic areas, or be used to reduce the lightness of white areas, drapes, table coverings, etc.

1

2

GAUZES

Lighting gauzes
The appearance of the gauze and subjects behind it can be changed considerably by lighting balance. Lamp 1 alone, the gauze appears as a solid plane. Surface painting or decoration shows up clearly. The subject is unseen. Lamp 2 alone, the gauze disappears. The subject appears, a little softened by the gauze. Surface painting is silhouetted. Lamp 3, added to rear-light the gauze, increases mistiness over the scene.

Lettering
Lettering can be supported on stretched gauze. 1, in a shop window; 2, in spectaculars.

125

Decorative Panels—Applications

Where attractive staging has to be achieved on a strictly limited budget, decorative panels are among the most useful utility scenic units.

Versatile and simple to use
Built on an open framework, these panels can form the basis of a number of imaginative staging layouts. Free-standing as individual units, panels may repeat or develop a decorative theme over the staging area. Multiples of the same unit can be redistributed in various positions and combinations, to create a fresh overall impression in a short time. A similar design in several sizes gives the opportunity for pseudo-perspective arrangements.

Panel heights of around 6-12 ft have proved adaptable. When interlinked or hinged, a series of panels can be combined to form a multiple screen. Such screens can in turn be grouped to form scenic masses.

Appearance variations
The visual effects created by the panels themselves can be varied through differences in tone, surface texture, surface patterns, shape, translucency, hue, pattern density, and so on. Stencilled patterns, perforated hardboard, imitation stained-glass motifs on a clear plastic, air-brushed gauze, and many other exploratory opportunities immediately spring to mind.

The appearance of the units can be altered further by changes in the lighting treatment of individual panels. Glass-fibre, for instance, can be lit to emphasise form, translucency or surface contouring, according to how it is illuminated. Perforated patterns may often be used to cast floor patterns and they can appear frontally lit, or in silhouette. Even these few examples remind us of how readily we can ring the changes on what are, fundamentally, quite rudimentary forms.

Suspended panels
Lightweight panels can be suspended by 'invisible' fish-line, nylon thread, or decorative cords with their lower ends attached to battens, tubular barrels, or stage weights. Heavier assemblies will require steel-cord suspension, cross-battens nailed to adjacent scenic units, or similarly secure fixing methods.

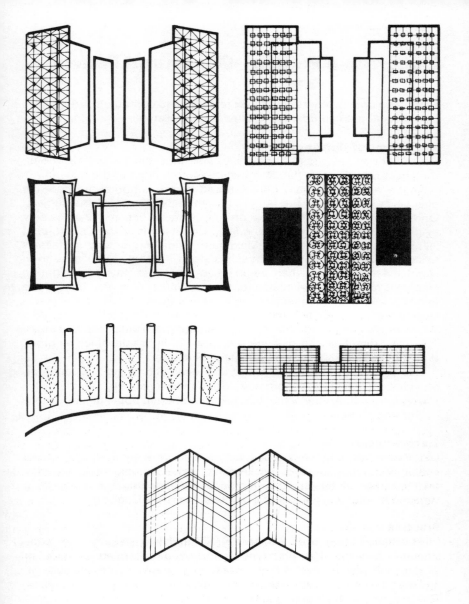

DECORATIVE PANELS – APPLICATIONS

Decorative panels
The entire staging can be derived from decorative panels, probably against an
open light or dark cyc.

127

Decorative Panels—Contoured Panels

Part of the attractiveness offered by textured and contoured surfaces lies
in the way light can be used to alter their appearance.

The effect of lighting
When light shines straight on to a surface from the camera viewpoint,
the effect is to create a flat, shadowless reproduction of the material.

As the lamp is gradually moved round from this frontal position, the
change in direction of the light, alters the appearance of the subject.
Undulations and prominences on the surface become increasingly
evident, as shadows lengthen and, in practical terms, surface contouring
is progressively emphasised. Maximum modelling of any surface is
usually obtained when the light skims along it obliquely because even
slight indentations are then emphasised. However, this edge lighting
emphasis may be far too coarse for the case in hand, so that instead we
need to choose an intermediate angle. Alternatively, it may be preferable
to maintain this steep lighting angle and control the modelling emphasis
with soft (diffuse) shadowless *fill light* to illuminate the shadowed areas.
The exact direction and balance (i.e. ratio) of light intensities required,
will depend upon the subject and its application.

This property of light to limn details of structure, texture, contour,
provides an exciting opportunity for the designer and, incidentally,
allows him to make the same item take on different appearances simply
by lighting changes.

Decorative wood
Decorative wooden panels can be devised with interestingly varied
characters : wooden slats, wickerwork, woven strips, bark, wooden
textures and, of course, the traditional architectural forms found in
wooden mouldings, linen-fold and other forms of panelling.

Plastics
Plastic panels have been explored in TV and film staging, with considerable success. The first type is the vacuum-formed product, in
which a thin plastic sheet is held close to a decorative contoured surface,
and then drawn down while warm and malleable, to take up these shapes.
The thin plastic shell that results may be self-coloured or painted and,
apart from unbelievably realistic reproductions of brick, stone, paving,
plasterwork, etc., this method is used to manufacture ornamental shapes.

The second type of plastic panel is solid, handworked and carved
(by hot wire, for example) from such materials as expanded polystyrene
(styrofoam) blocks and sheet. The ultra-lightweight material may
be used both in fretted stencil forms, or as sculpted relief, with equal
success.

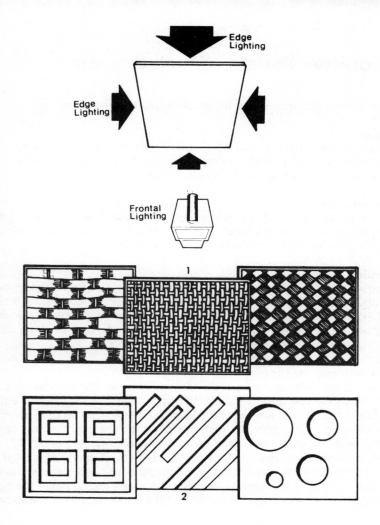

DECORATIVE PANELS – CONTOURED PANELS

Lighting and modelling
The prominence of modelling and texture changes with the lighting angle. Oblique lighting gives greatest contouring and textural emphasis whereas light from the camera direction produces flat results.

Textural surfaces
1, Contoured panels can be constructed from interwoven wood ; 2, Screens can be made from multi-layer and strongly modelled, forms using wooden shapes, or from plastic shell motifs.

Decorative Panels—Mesh Screens

Mesh has both decorative and utilitarian applications in staging.

Netting
Fishnet or garden netting can be draped or stretched over a frame of timber or metal tubing. Drape frames themselves might be pressed into service here, as a framework for hanging objects.

Mesh screens
Horticultural plastic mesh comes in various dimensions, and can be used to construct firm mesh screens, with a certain amount of contouring and folding to introduce interesting structural formations.

Expanded metal
Expanded metal sheeting is of a much stiffer nature, and therefore more able to support items hung upon it (page 132). A somewhat less flexible material, metal mesh cannot be 'draped' in ways possible with lighter ones, but it does permit shaping into rigid rubular or rectangular forms, such as pillars or similar vertical constructions.

Modifying appearance
Although these mesh screen panels can be used directly in such varied forms, much can be done to alter their appearance or decorate them. Fish-nets, for example, are transformed by applying silver or gold spray. When they are further adorned with creeper and blossom, the nets can lose their identity completely, and take on new decorative potential.

Even mundane, routine mesh can be painted, shaded, or colour-sprayed and given a fresh look. Economically minded people have achieved a double advantage by backing the mesh with a panel during spraying, and so decorated this surface with a mesh pattern at the same time !

Finally, we can modify the appearance of mesh screens by facing them on their front or rear sides with coloured media such as gelatin, translucent plastic sheeting or glass-fibre strips. Similarly, fabric drapes, foliage, intertwined foils, can be applied to this foundation.

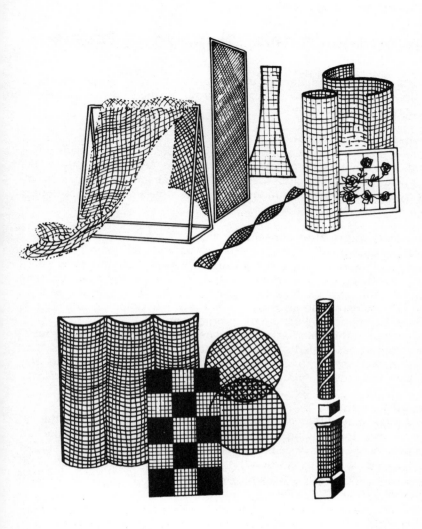

DECORATIVE PANELS – MESH SCREENS

Mesh units

Mesh units are an adaptable concept. They can be formed from netting or wire, displayed in silhouette, or directly lit, and arranged in sculptural, architectural and draped forms.

Decorative Panels—Supported Panels

Panels can be introduced for an effective display of large decorative motifs, particularly where these would prove too flimsy or complicated to suspend in free-hanging form.

Translucent hung panel
Translucent hung panels are very suitable for illuminated effects. A symbol that is unseen behind such a panel is revealed on cue as the fitting is lit. Flashing signs can be developed in this manner as, for example, where a stencil arranged on 'frosted' plastic sheeting is lit from the rear with vari-coloured light.

Vertically supported screens
Vertically supported screens can be placed within a setting to display large graphics such as maps, drawings or enlarged photographs. These can, in fact, provide the entire scenery for a speaker—an appropriate environment, perhaps, for a talk, lecture, interview, or similar presentation. The cameras can also shoot the screens as graphics, totally or as selected sections, to illustrate the programme.

Developing this idea further, the panels might serve for the layout of a number of associated graphics, photographs, etc. The cameras then have instant access to whichever is required, in any order, and may explore them (by zooming, tracking, panning) at a moment's notice.

Support methods
Decorative motifs that are strongly constructed can be supported in free space by top hanging, and tensioned by bottom-edge lines attached to floor weights. Heavy or bulky items need steel cables (preferably of similar tone to the background) while for lightweight subjects, thin nylon line may suffice, additional side support lines being fitted if necessary, to obviate sway.

DECORATIVE PANELS – SUPPORTED PANELS

Supported motifs
Large decorative motifs can be suspended.

Supported screens
Supported screens can complement other staging.

Photo-murals
Suspended photographic enlargements provide effective staging and also
'caption material' for close-up cameras.

Flexible Screens

Flexible screens offer certain unusual staging opportunities, because their effective shapes can be changed quite quickly and simply.

Construction
These screens can be made from hinged metal strips, or from a series of close, parallel wooden laths fixed to a fabric backing. In principle akin to the flexible security shutters used to protect shop fronts, these screens are set up on edge, usually as self-supporting units.

Adaptability
They can be arranged in various interesting forms. Rolled up, they become pillars, unrolled, they might be convex, concave, or S-shaped to suit the situation.

Such screens are conveniently rolled and stored, and can be supplemented by other scenic units, so that they may offer useful economic variations for small studio staging.

Decorative variations
If provided with different coverings or tones on either face, the appearance of the flexible screens may be altered further. Controlled lighting on their undulating surfaces may change the contrast, tone, or hue.

The flexible screen has the advantage, too, of not normally being visually associated with other objects, and has been used effectively as a background for talks, dance routines, demonstrations, and a variety of other programmes. As graphics or decorative motifs can be attached to the screens, they are surpringly adaptable within their limits.

FLEXIBLE SCREENS

These can be used singly or combined, in various curved shapes.

Convincing to the eye, convenient for the camera.

Floor Treatment—Painting

The floor of most TV studios is a precision-laid surface; flat, even-toned, level, non-skid, hard-wearing, slightly resilient, acoustically suitable to dampen noise. The floor often comprises a matte neutral lino or allied material, on a wood block foundation. Such precautions are necessary to provide smooth camera movement. This flooring surface has proved highly adaptable, and is readily redecorated. Applied by a large roller and removed by machine-scrubbing, water-soluble paints have the advantage of rapid, easy coverage. Their drawback is that accidental water spillage can result in hazardous, slippery conditions.

Simulated effects
Floors can be painted by a scenic artist using any of the methods outlined on page 48. So the floor surface can give the impression to the camera of texture, shading, tonal variations and can also be decorated to simulate paving slabs, cobbles, earth, carpets, chequer-board patterns, tiles, etc. To assist hand treatment by artists, stencils may be used such as for parquet flooring block patterns.

Network studios employ floor-printing machines fitted with large, replaceable rubber rollers to provide certain routine floor decoration. These would include paving, cobbles, floor blocks and planking.

Painted textural effects are convenient to apply, and avoid the picture-judder that uneven flooring introduces. They are not convincing in really close shots however, tend to disappear under concentrated backlight reflections, and smear or wipe off if wetted.

Decorative motifs
Large decorative floor motifs may be created by 'stick and rip' methods. Here, designs are formed from shaped plastic tape and sheet which are temporarily fixed to the floor while being overpainted. The adhesive materials are then removed to leave a painted floor pattern.

Large areas of floor are quite often blackened for low-key effects. However, dark even floor tones can show footmarks, tyre marks, and scuffs, and may need refurbishing before the recording or transmission session.

High gloss floors can be effective, provided that their shiny surfaces do not reflect lamps. Strong specular reflections generally leave the TV camera at a disadvantage, and produce blocked-off white 'streaking' across the picture, 'lag effects' (ectoplasmically trailing), video overload, hot spots, and similar visual disturbances. The lighting treatment might have to be arranged specifically to avoid these defects, rather than for optimum pictorial effect.

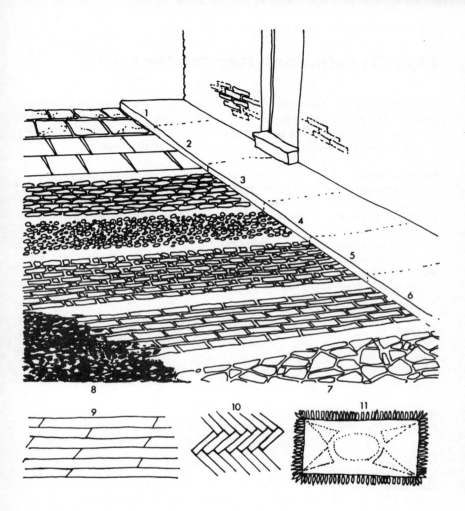

FLOOR TREATMENT – PAINTING

Floor painting can suggest a wide range of materials.

Exterior floor painting

1, Paving slabs – worn; 2, New paving; 3, Cobbles; 4, Irregular stones; 5, Stone sets; 6, Pave; 7, Crazy paving; 8, Broken earth.

Interior floor painting

9, Wood-plank flooring; 10, Parquet flooring; 11, Painted carpet.

Floor Treatment—Applied Pattern

Particularly where elaborate floor designs are concerned, a considerable amount of studio time may be saved if one can prepare it elsewhere, and fit it during the scenic setting period. This avoids the usual dilemma of work cessation while wet, freshly painted flooring dries.

Floor cloths
The appearance of the floor area can be changed by laying large decorated floor cloths of hessian, duck, or other heavy duty fabrics. However, there are limitations to this method. It is not easy to achieve a completely smooth, crease-free surface. Accurate positioning takes time and geometrical patterns too easily distort. Cameras may move over the surface without undue picture-bumping, but are liable to pull and wrinkle the floor cloth in the process, even when the edges have been taped to the floor by adhesive fabric or plastic tape to try and overcome this.

Tapes
Tapes can be used also to build-up decorative floor patterns particularly for spiders' webs or geometric shapes. So also, plastic sheeting, or even wallpaper, can be stuck to the floor, where little wear is anticipated.

Prepared board
Patterns may be painted onto prepared board or light card, which is then laid on the studio floor and anchored by double-sided adhesive tape.

Carpets
Carpets can be used as a floor covering in any staging area as long as camera dollies and sound booms do not have to move over them. It is usually practicable to remove carpeting or roll it aside, where equipment access is required for particular shots. Most sound engineers welcome carpet, particularly in smaller settings, to reduce spurious foot noises, and to improve the rather hollow, live acoustics that such surroundings produce (page 160).

FLOOR TREATMENT – APPLIED PATTERNS

Floor cloths

A decorated floor cloth provides patterning that can be removed quickly, and also re-used.

Surface decoration

Floor decoration can be provided by 1, Laid-down strips ; 2, Painted design ; 3, Stuck-on areas.

Floor Treatment—Lighting

Light offers boundless opportunities for attractive decorative floor patterning. But this calls for facilities, time—and sometimes considerable patience.

Methods

We can create decorative patterns either as *cast shadows* (where a lamp throws shadows of a large stencil cut-out), or as *projected light patterns* from specially-designed lamp fittings (effects projector, scenic projector).

For successful cast shadows, we must ensure that there is an appreciable lamp-to-stencil distance in order to obtain a sharp shadow pattern, and use a small intense point light source that can be operated vertically.

Optically projected patterns, on the other hand, are more conveniently adjusted. But projector light outputs are often quite limited, or the resultant pattern size too small. Larger projected patterns require either a wider angle projector lens (shorter focal length), or a longer *throw* (lamp to surface distance). Either of these reduces the light pattern brightness obtained.

Problems

So much for methods. What are the problems? There are several, and they apply equally to all decorative light projection (e.g. for light patterns on walls).

Surfaces should be light toned, matte, and unpatterned. Light patterns are not successful on dark, shiny, decorated areas.

No scenery, hung equipment, etc., should interrupt the light beam.

Ideally, light projection should be at right angles to the surface, otherwise there is distortion and lack of sharpness in places. Projection usually has to be obliquely angled in practice.

Where an overall effect is devised from a series of adjacent light patterns, accurate matching and blending is mechanically an extremely exacting process.

Any lamp movement (i.e. lamp swing) will disturb projected patterns. Performers may move into light beams and become unsuitably lit. Properly lit performer-areas cannot normally be arranged within a light patterned floor area. Portrait lighting interferes with the light pattern, and vice versa.

Light rays themselves are only visible in smoky, foggy, or steamy surroundings. Studio ventilation usually frustrates 'light streaming through leaded windows' and similar effects. Instead, a 'cheated' method such as defocused superimposed graphics, may be preferable.

Many spotlights and projectors cannot be used vertically without over-heating and early burn-out.

1

3

2

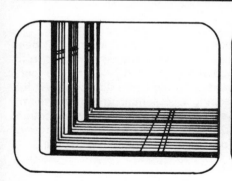

FLOOR TREATMENT -- LIGHTING

Projected light patterns
Light patterns can be used : 1, combined, or 2, individually, to create a staging effect. Spotlights can produce isolated pools of light 3.

Cast shadow patterns
Scenic units can provide cast shadows. These may be augmented artificially by painted simulation.

Floor Treatment—Surface Covering

Scattering is probably the quickest and simplest way of obscuring the floor for scenic effect, the required material being thrown in strategic places, to supplement other treatment (floor painting, surface build-up, grass, etc.).

Scatter materials

Typical acceptable substances include:
1. *Peat*—to suggest soil, dirty conditions.
2. *Sawdust*—for snow, sand or earth (in its white, fawn, and sometimes dark brown forms).
3. *Cork chips*—provides 'quiet gravel' (real gravel crunches noisily on mic., and may be hazardous).
4. *Expanded polystyrene granules, shredded paper*—can sometimes be used for snowy areas (but may prove too white).
5. *Dry leaves*—strewn to add conviction to rural exteriors.

The main considerations for all floor scattering materials is that they should not be a fire risk, they should not foul-up equipment (get into cameras, lamps or clog under wheels), should not blow around (avoid wind-machines, fans, etc.), and should be inert, non-corrosive and non-abrasive (so salt and sand are forbidden for scenic use).

Floor protection

Protective tarpaulin or plastic sheeting spread on the ground can help to keep the studio floor surface clean, prevent scattered materials from spreading, and aid clearing-up operations. Remember that the performer's feet can tread these materials onto the clean floor area left for camera operations, so regular sweeping is essential to confine them. Wheels (and people) can easily skid on the residue. Tyres acquire stuck-on lumps! Particularly try to avoid wetting any floor-scattered materials. The sludge that results from this can be harder to handle.

Floor covering

Certain floor surface coverings need to be imitated by artist painting or by specially devised substitutes. Real paving slabs, for example, are too heavy to use en masse because of handling, storage and floor loading problems. Consequently, one uses:
1. Sheets or mats of rubber or plastic for cobbles or tiles.
2. Glass-fibre paving slabs for pavements (suitably raised on low platforms with internal sound-deadening sacks—e.g. sawdust).
3. Grass matting—irregularly shaded for more realistic effect. Turf can be laid, but is heavy and time consuming.

There are times when only the real thing will do (e.g. a floor of laid planking) to convey the right sounds or satisfy close shots. Then the designer may have no alternative but to lay a restricted area with these materials, taking care not to damage the studio floor in the process.

FLOOR TREATMENT – SURFACE COVERING

Surface covering

Various materials transform surfaces convincingly. 1, A standard flat ; 2, plastic shell is attached to the flat simulating brickwork, stone, etc ; 3, Glass fibre paving slabs are on a timber foundation ; 4, Acoustical damping is provided by sawdust sacks ; 5, Glass fibre kerb stones ; 6, Rubber cobble stone sheets ; 7, Scattered peat ; 8, Stretched grass matting ; 9, Grass mat over sawdust bags ; 10, 'Sand pile' of sawdust.

143

Floor Treatment—Height Variation

The flat studio floor is fine for most staging purposes, but can be scenically unrealistic for situations representing exterior locations. To provide variations in floor height, a number of well-tried methods have been evolved.

Hillocks and craters

Irregularities such as hillocks can be built up with scenic blocks, timber framework, ramps, tightly-packed closed sawdust sacks. Sandbags are heavy, but most effective for devising firm ramparts and mounds.

More elevated areas can be assembled from vari-height rostra (parallels), or specially built erections of tubular scaffolding.

When holes in the ground or depressed areas are required, the solution lies in building up the surrounding floor level overall with rostra, leaving the lower level where necessary. This technique is introduced wherever it is essential to have people walk downstairs, use trapdoors, go down wells, and to simulate graves, bomb craters or digging operations.

Faking the situation

Sometimes it is possible to 'dummy' action to suggest that a situation exists instead of providing actual conditions. An actor may walk up to a dummy or unbacked door to open it, the director cutting at that moment to the next shot. Similarly, a trapdoor opening away from the camera can be raised without it being seen that there is no corresponding hole in the studio floor. People have even 'walked downstairs' behind a screen, by progressively bending their knees as they went!

Technical problems

If cameras have to move around on elevated areas, these surfaces must be suitably prepared so that they are level, flat, non-skid and reinforced. Wherever heavy staging or equipment has to be supported, properly constructed tubular scaffolding becomes essential to ensure load safety.

Rostra can provide problems for the sound engineer. Footsteps are, likely to sound unnaturally hollow as they resonate. To reduce the noise the rostrum-top can be surfaced with felt, foam plastic sheeting, cork-chip faced felting, and internally packed with sawdust bags.

Rocks

Rocks are generally formed from timber foundations covered with expanded wire having a suitably painted canvas or glass-fibre skin, or carved expanded polystyrene blocks. Plastic shell mouldings may similarly suggest outcropping rock formations or uneven ground. Unless specifically constructed for climbing over, these areas are only suitable as scenic effects.

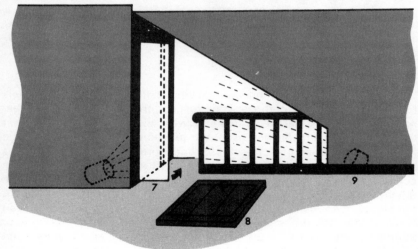

FLOOR TREATMENT – HEIGHT VARIATION

Hillocks and holes

Holes in the ground are created within built-up rostra (platforms). 1, Contoured flat as rock ; 2, Irregular ground from painted tarpaulin ; 3, Earth (peat), sand (sawdust) ; 4, Profiled cut-out horizon ; 5, Rostra ; 6, Hole in rostrum top.

Dummy substitutes

Indirect staging approaches can convey the idea that there is a lower floor, although none exists. 7, Ground lamp behind door, suggests a cellar ; 8, Dummy trap door, a wooden surround frame with lifting trap ; 9, Hidden ground lamp suggests, from light direction and shadows, a hall below.

General Staging—Rooms

Although set designing is a highly skilled and sensitively perceptive process, a careful examination of staging patterns or layouts reveals a number of regularly recurrent themes.

How regular staging approaches evolve
There are several very good reasons for this. A high proportion of TV staging represents the interiors of everyday dwellings, offices, public buildings, etc. These places follow recognisable architectural conventions. If we disregard these familiar forms during staging, the result is either architecturally improbable, or strangely unconventional. In any normal interior, we shall find furniture disposed in a series of customary positions. The way people would be expected to use this location, itself follows a predictable pattern; they invariably enter doors, sit at tables, look out of windows, and so on. We find, moreover, that for most TV shows there are optimum camera angles that shoot each of these actions to best advantage.

So, although a particular arrangement has been created to suit a specific show, we can often discern familiar patterns in both the staging and camera treatment used. Certain types of interior, in fact, are seen quite regularly.

Typical themes
Looking closely at these layouts, we find that there are usually well-founded productional purposes, too; for the furniture positions we see. A downstage desk, parallel with a side wall, allows cross-shooting that would be less practicable in other positions. Isolated downstage furniture provides scope for useful full-face foreground shots, and gives depth. Generally speaking, upstage action furniture introduces various complications in production mechanics (e.g. cameras need to move upstage within the setting, or use camera traps to achieve close shots). Fireplaces form handy action focal points, as people stand or lean beside them. Windows are an asset, not only in conveying 'day' or 'night' instantly, but their backings imply an external environment, that people can look out onto — a garden; a roof-top vista.

There are regular situations, too, that can affect staging treatment. For example, low foreground viewpoints of people positioned downstage, call for precautions against shooting over the distant walls. Upstage cameras shooting people at side wall locations, or seated downstage, are liable to shoot off past the downstage edges of the set. So some form of edge-masking becomes necessary.

Here we have just a few instances of the essential relationships between staging treatment for pictorial effect, and the demands made by the mechanics of production. The set designer is a creative artist, but one with a firmly-based realisation of practical studio requirements.

146

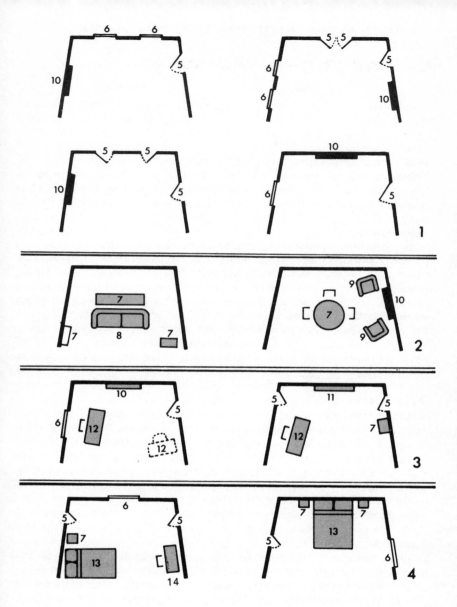

GENERAL STAGING – ROOMS

Recurrent basic staging patterns

Architectural layouts tend to be recurrent. Furniture too follows recognisable
positions, so when action and camera treatment have been decided, certain
features become familiar. The patterns shown here are :
1, Lounge architecture. 2, Lounge furniture. 3, Office. 4, Bedroom. 5, Door.
6, Window. 7, Table. 8, Settee. 9, Armchair. 10, Fireplace. 11, Bookcase.
12, Desk. 13, Bed. 14, Dressing table.

General Staging—Work Areas

In televised demonstrations, each subject makes its own particular staging demands. Some are best shot from a distance, with intercut close-ups to point detail ; others require close and ultra-close production treatment throughout. Staging for work areas must be adaptable, and on a scale appropriate to the programme.

Various services may be called for, including electrical power supplies (using isolating transformers for safety), piped water, drainage, or even load-bearing hoists, steam, compressed air, floor-anchoring points.

Adaptability

Tables, benches, or similar working surfaces are important adjuncts for most demonstrations. We can increase the height of existing units by legging up (adding bottom extensions) or blocking up (page 100).

Individual items can be raised on small wooden or plastic blocks where necessary. So a camera could take level shots of a blocked-up glass vessel to watch chemical action, and yet still look down into dishes on the table surface. Miniature blocks and strips (e.g. $\frac{1}{2}$ in to 3 in high) assist in propping articles, to tilt them towards the camera.

Mirrors give shot variety where necessary (page 58) to show aspects of the subject that would not otherwise be visible—to look downwards into a pan of food, or upwards beneath a car, perhaps. If a considerable proportion of the production involves such extreme viewpoints, it may be preferable to anticipate this in the staging. A camera tower can facilitate high shots. For continual low shots, the entire staging could be set up on rostra (parallels). Each has its drawbacks, though. The former ties the camera to a fixed point. In the latter, floor cameras might not achieve sufficiently elevated positions for their other shots in the area.

Action points in a programme may be centralised, or diversified around a number of separate positions. Design can reflect this by unifying staging treatment, or by creating continuous decor between areas.

Graphics

The set designer may also be concerned with the supply or co-ordination of graphics for the show. Fundamentally, these may be introduced in three ways. They may be interposed by the director as cut-in pictures—from slides, film, video tape or shots from other cameras. They can be presented as an integral part of the setting—stuck-on flats, slipped into wall openings, rear projected or electronically inserted on wall screens, shown on a TV monitor screen. Finally, graphics can be directly handled by the demonstrator himself, so creating greater participation. The range here is very extensive, and includes hold-up cards, book displays, and various graphics build-up processes—blackboard, over-head projector, stick-on details (magnetic or tacky-backed), operating animated captions, illuminated panels, etc.

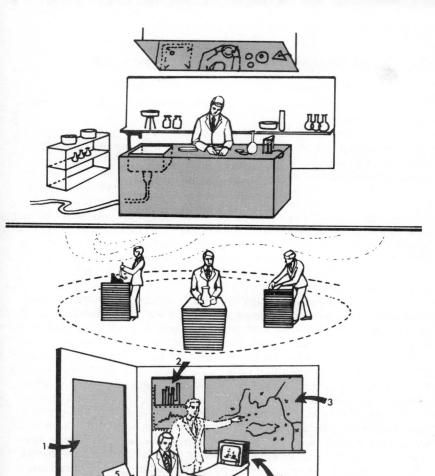

GENERAL STAGING – WORK AREAS

Facilities
A demonstration may require a range of facilities (e.g. water, drainage, gas and electricity supplies). An overhead mirror may help to give a clearer viewpoint.

Overall decor
Where there is a series of isolated work areas in a production, appropriate staging can unify them, to prevent a disjointed long shot.

Display area
The staging gives maximum opportunities for displayed graphics to illustrate talks. 1, Rear projection screen and chroma-key background ; 2, Wall graphics area (with magnetic/adhesive surface) ; 3, Area for large maps, photo-enlargements, etc. ; 4, Picture monitor for cueing ; 5, Table caption holder.

General Staging—Musical Groups

The presentation of musical groups on television usually follows certain regular patterns :
1. Solos—Solo singers, solo instrumentalists.
2. Small groups—Instrumental groups, backing groups of singers, musical combinations (combos), pop groups.
3. Large groups—Choirs, bands, orchestras.

Televised music brings its own particular and very practical problems for the designer. For much of the time, the production director is concerned largely with the performers' expressions, instrumental techniques, and similar close-up detail. Only occasionally will he move cameras out to take a wide, overall view, to reveal the full staging treatment, and only then will the designer have the opportunity for broad scenic effect.

Staging mechanics
The mechanics of group staging are often complicated by two factors. Firstly, the amount of space people and their instruments take up necessarily determine the floor area required. Secondly, however we might be tempted to split groups apart into localised segments (e.g. an orchestra into its sub-sections) for visual effect, or to improve camera access, there are dangers that one might disrupt their internal musical balance and spoil the performance. A soloist is unable to hear an accompaniment, or see the conductor. From such facts, conventions grow.

In staging for *soloists*, we can emphasise their isolation, and concentrate attention with a podium, floor pattern, or spotlight; provide a naturalistic setting (e.g. a music room) ; or scenic features (e.g. a staircase, furniture or floral displays) as visual centres for their movements.

Smaller musical groups are often presented on-stepped or raised areas to display them more effectively, and allow more varied viewpoints for cameras. For large groups, safety considerations are particularly important, and in addition to ensuring rigidity and strength in rostra, edgeboards and rails should be fitted to prevent accidents.

Simplicity is often the keyword
Attractive visual effects can be achieved from quite simple staging. A mid-grey cyc and floor (with a cove or ground row) can form the basis for a diversity of styles. Columns, decorative panels, etc., can be set up against it. Results can be arresting, and yet the expense minimal.

Imaginative lighting offers considerable potential when staging musical productions. Its flexibility, its facility for atmospheric and decorative changes are almost unlimited. So structural staging, as such, may often be kept to a minimum.

Sometime staging is deliberately devised to incorporate 'acoustic screens', that by their sound-absorbent or reflective properties can help to reinforce or isolate sound areas, to enhance acoustical quality.

GENERAL STAGING – MUSICAL GROUPS

Isolation
Isolation may prevent a soloist and accompanying musicians from hearing and seeing each other sufficiently well.

Sub-division
Physically subdividing an orchestra may achieve more varied shots, but affect the orchestra's coordination.

Acoustic screens
Screens may be introduced both to produce attractive pictures and to improve the acoustical quality of staging.

Scenic Projection

Scenic projection can be either from the front or rear, with displays ranging from simple light and shadow patterns, to photographic slides.

Rear projection

Basic rear projection uses a translucent sheet (plastic or linen) illuminated from behind, and displaying silhouetted patterns, shadows and reflections (e.g. from metal-foil shapes). Decorative motifs, stencils, foliage and suspended items of all kinds, can be used; sometimes being given movement by cords, fans or motors.

A more advanced form of rear projection (Back projection, B.P.) displays photographic slides of graphics, titling, pictorial locations, etc. A properly-designed process-screen material is preferable for optimum results; viz. to prevent undue light absorption or an uneven image. Smaller screens may be used as display surfaces in a setting, or even as limited scenic backings (e.g. outside windows).

Large professional rear-projection screens are often 10-20 ft wide, specially manufactured of plastic sheet stretched on a frame. For such large images, the projector needs to be a high-output precision model, requiring a screen-to-projector distance of some 20-40 ft. A large intermediate vertical mirror often proves necessary to bend the light path, and so confine the set-up.

Both motion picture and TV studios have made considerable use of large-screen rear-projection to augment staging, or to provide the total scenic background behind performers. Still slides or moving film can be projected, and at its best, the result is totally convincing.

Against the relative cheapness, flexibility and simplicity of this facility, are the practical problems involved—image dilution by spill-light, uneven clarity and brightness, the limitations of shooting angle (image distortion, light fall-off), and various associated technical problems relative to lighting, sound and camera movement. Acting areas or foreground staging should rarely be permitted within 6 ft of the screen face.

Front projection

In the simple version, images are projected on to any light scenic surface; a technique usually confined to lighting effects (page 116) and small displays, due to the distortion and image-dilution incurred.

A much superior facility has found increasing application. Known as *reflex projection* (front axial projection), this employs a special beaded screen, having the property of reflecting a brilliant, undistorted image over a very narrow angle. The picture projector shoots along the camera lens axis directly onto the screen, the camera seeing the reflected scene and the foreground performers combined in a single image. As always, the realism relies upon good matching (of perspective, scale, brightness, colour, lighting, etc.).

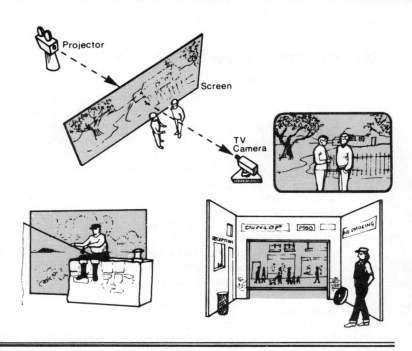

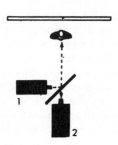

SCENIC PROJECTION

Rear projection

The image from a slide or film projector is focused onto a matte translucent
screen. The TV camera sees foreground action as if within the background scene.
Unlike reflex projection or electronic projection methods, the camera can often move
or zoom to adjust shot size, without incongruous effects.

Reflex projection

The projector image 1, is reflected by the 45° glass sheet onto a multi-beaded
screen. The bright picture and the foreground subject are together seen by the
TV camera 2, through the glass.

153

Electronic Picture Insertion

By ingenious electronic switching, it is possible to intimately mix two televised pictures so that the subject of one shot appears within a background scene provided by a second camera or picture source. For the set designer, this means that part or all of the scenic treatment may be produced from slides, stills, motion pictures, drawings, paintings, models, video-tape, or pictures from other studio cameras.

Problems arise in matching the subject and background shots in tone, contrast, light direction, colour, scale, perspective, etc. Spurious mixing or 'breakthrough' may arise. The insertion process is usually only suitable for one camera set-up at a time. But by careful planning and experience these limitations are contained.

Electronic picture insertion has been applied variously to provide total background scenes, to insert locations 'outside' the windows of rooms and automobiles, and to create abstract effects.

Types of insertion
Considering its versatility, the basic principles of electronic insertion are absurdly simple. There are two fundamental methods.*
1. *External key matte.* Here, wherever an area of one picture is masked off (matted) the corresponding part of another TV picture appears instead. This mask may be adjusted to be of any size, shape or position, and can be created mechanically (A), or electronically (B). It can be applied to localised areas (e.g. a window in the studio is inserted into that part of a painted scene). Masking can also be used to create ornamental cut-out shapes or divisions of the picture or to provide a 'split-screen' effect, or again, to give picture-transition 'wipes'.
2. *Self-keying.* In the second insertion system, a specific tone (C) or colour (D) in the master camera scene operates an electronic switch. Wherever this device 'sees' the switching clue in the master shot, it automatically suppresses picture in the master camera, and transmits instead a second video source (the slave, or background picture). In the combined treated picture, we see the subject completely integrated into the background scene.

This automatic switching enables a person in front of the master camera to walk around in the background scene (but not normally to pass 'behind' objects). In the masked area matte system, free movement is only possible within the masked section of the picture.

It also permits automatic *infill* of tone, texture or colour into graphics (e.g. caption lettering). In colour TV, hues can be generated entirely electronically (with a *colour synthesiser*), and these colours may be introduced similarly as plain colour infill for lettering, caption background, or even to replace normal picture tones.

*A, Camera matte, inlay mask; B, Special effects generator (SEG), keyed insertion; C, Luminance keying; D, Chroma-key, CSO (colour separation overlay).

154

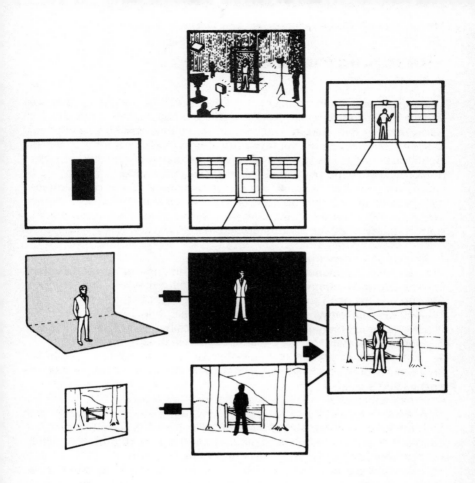

ELECTRONIC PICTURE INSERTION

External key
Wherever a masking area is positioned in the insertion apparatus (mechanically or electronically) only that part of the studio scene before the subject camera will be inserted into the corresponding area of the background picture.

Self-keying (self-matting)
The subject must be placed in front of a specially chosen surface (keying or switching tone or hue). Wherever this keying tone or hue appears in the master shot, and it must be avoided in the subject itself, the background scene appears instead, in the composite picture.

155

The Influence of Lighting

The appearance of most subjects becomes substantially changed as the relative angle and intensity of light falling upon surfaces are altered. Appearance is modified, too, according to whether this light is diffused (*soft*) or of a clear-cut shadow-producing (*hard*) character. We can alter the pictorial effect of staging very considerably by lighting approaches. The same place may be made to look crude, rich, gay, sad, depressing, lit by daylight or localised luminants, have a three-dimensional or flat construction, according to the choice of lighting treatment. Whether time, facilities and production mechanics permit such a variety of effect, is another matter.

Lighting provides opportunities

We can only summarise here the very fundamental opportunities that lighting provides, relative to creative staging, but they are a reminder of the approaches open to the lighting director. Light can:
1. Shift attention towards specific areas with subtlety or directness.
2. Reveal detail, texture or form sympathetically or with coarseness.
3. Emphasise detail, texture or form, delicately or strongly.
4. Conceal detail, texture or form, obliterating it or subduing it gently.
5. Imply that subjects exist (e.g. a window shadow where no window or wall exists).
6. Provide colour.
7. Modify existing colour.
8. Influence our interpretation of size, scale, space or distance.
9. Concentrate on outline, and suppress surface contouring and detail (*silhouette*).
10. Concentrate on surface detail, suppressing surface contouring (notan).
11. Create compositional relationships.
12. Falsely suggest contour where none exists (e.g. by shading, by shadows).
13. Establish mood, atmosphere or time, where no other indications exist.
14. Create visual isolation, or suggest spatial continuity.
15. Create an environment by associative treatment.
16. Reveal or conceal translucency.
17. Create decorative patterns of illumination.
18. Create decorative shadow effects.

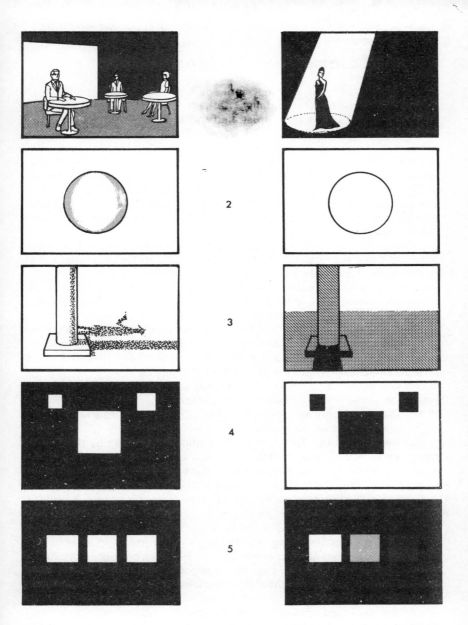

THE INFLUENCE OF LIGHTING

The effect of light

1, Light can direct attention, subtly or strongly ; 2, it can reveal form or obliterate it ; 3, it can reveal or conceal that subjects exist ; 4, it influences our impression of size, and 5, affects our assessment of distance.

157

Lighting is concerned with optimised portraiture, as well as pictorial effect.
Staging can inadvertently impair both.

Typical Lighting Problems

Because staging has a direct influence upon the effectiveness of lighting, and upon picture quality, we have suggested here the various ways in which these can be frustrated by scenic design. These are not rules advocating foolproof unadventurous staging techniques, but reminders as to how pictorial impact can be blunted by oversight.

Tone—One generally aims to limit tones in staging, furniture, properties, clothing. Surface reflectance should not exceed 70% (Munsell 8·5), or fall below $3\frac{1}{2}$% (Munsell 2·5) if it is to be controllable. High contrast in large adjacent areas in the picture is particularly undesirable. Lighting invariably increases tonal contrast anyway—possibly beyond the TV system's tonal limits.

Surface—Shiny surfaces strongly reflect lighting. Dark shiny areas may develop distracting hot-spots long before the illumination is sufficient to reveal their detail and contouring.

All near-horizontal surfaces reflect backlight and, if smooth, are liable to appear over-bright, whatever their tone. Rougher surfaces are less prone to such bounce, even when light-toned.

Glass in pictures, windows, furniture and similarly highly reflective surfaces are specially liable to reflect lighting and create picture defects.

Set heights—Sets should not be built higher than needed for the production. Steep lighting is pictorially unattractive.

Set positions—The positions and distribution of staging should be related to all technical facilities, safety factors, etc.

Set shapes—Confined, unsplayed, shallow, or long narrow layouts can aggravate operational problems.

Lighting treatment—Treatment is essentially influenced by the equipment, time, and space available. Certain lighting techniques require specific conditions to be effective (e.g. light-patterns may be precluded by insufficiently powerful lamps, limited space, intervening scenery, etc.).

Backings—Backings should not be too close to scenic openings (e.g. 6 ft minimum for small areas).

Windows—Frosted, opaque, or fully curtained windows frequently provide blank, unconvincing results. Translucent, decorative windows (hammered or rolled glass or stained glass) require a strongly illuminated plain light-toned backing beyond them, rather than direct lighting through them. Only clear unobstructed windows provide distinct wall patterns.

Cycloramas—Cyc cloths should be clean, undamaged, and hung without wrinkles for optimum lighting. Staging should be displaced from the cyc to avoid accidental shadowing.

Practical lamps—All practical electric fittings should be earthed. Hung practicals should be arranged to avoid distracting shadows on people and the setting. Upstage areas are typically safest.

Ceilings—All ceilings should be included only after close consultation with the director and the lighting specialist involved.

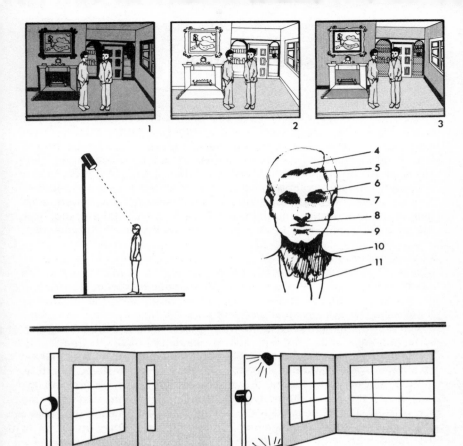

TYPICAL LIGHTING PROBLEMS

Scenic tones
Scenic tones can be 1, too dark and unrelieved overall, or 2, too light, and unaccented, for attractive pictorial effects. A more successful tonal balance, 3, includes a well-defined range of tones giving appropriate accent and variety.

Steep lighting
Aggravated by high flats or scenic restriction, steep lighting angles produce ugly portraiture. Common defects include : 4, Hot top to head ; 5, Hair dark at front ; 6, Black eye-sockets ; 7, Ears light at top, dark within ; 8, Nose shadow over entire top lip ; 9, Lower lip shadow ; 10, Neck in deep shadow ; 11, Head shadow on chest.

Close backings
Where backings are close to scenic openings, both interior and exterior lighting is degraded.

Typical Sound Problems

Oversimplifying, one could say that the main preoccupations of the TV audio man (sound engineer) are in ensuring that the relative volume and quality of sounds match the situation suggested by the picture. If the shot shows a cave, then the sound should be appropriately reverberant. On a hilltop, dead open-air sound is essential for the illusion. People who are close to the camera should be heard more loudly and more clearly than someone who is more distant (this is termed *sound perspective*). This adjustment to sound balance and quality has to be achieved, irrespective of the acoustic conditions that actually prevail in the studio. Both the cave and hilltop may have been electronically-inserted photo stills !

Incongruities
Staging can present audio problems when the acoustics or sound coloration it provides is incongruous. Where people ascend 'stone steps' to the hollow sound of thumping timber structures, the illusion is shattered. The set designer can improve matters by structural reinforcement, by filling hollow units with sawdust or plastic foam bags, by surfacing steps and rostra with sound-deadening materials (page144).

Sometimes the acoustics of small rooms can be improved by breaking up straight walls (by wall cabinets, jogs, etc.), by upholstered furniture, by floor carpeting, to subdue the otherwise hard, 'boxy' sound quality.

Some of the most impressive visual staging is quite disappointing acoustically. The fierce wind (from a wind machine) shaking the foliage of an 'exterior' scene, is just a low, rumbling 'wind on mic' obtrusion to the audio man, who is using tape or discs of the natural sound for realism. Similarly, a 'rain on window' effect may be convincing but sound like water dripping into a bucket as a floor rain-trough collects the falling spray. Sound and staging must be co-ordinated.

The sound boom
In most studios, a *sound boom* is used for general audio pick-up. The microphone at the end of its long telescopic pole is held near the performers, moving with them to suit the shot. This counter-balanced boom arm is pivoted on a movable pram. The boom operator on his platform swings and extends the arm, tilting and turning the mic towards the sound source.

Staging can thwart the proper operation of this sound boom unless arranged with sound pick-up in mind. Hanging devices such as practical lamps, hung motifs, foliage as well as such structural features as low arches, beams, columns, can impede the microphone or boom-arm moves. If floor structures or staging are congested, the boom may not have sufficient space to work in, being unable to contract ('rack-back') or swing the arm with its rear counterweight. So sound boom access is an important operational factor to be considered.

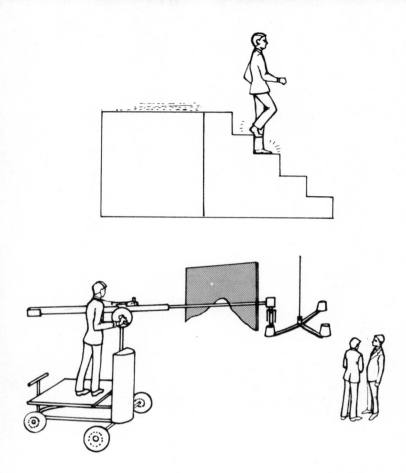

TYPICAL SOUND PROBLEMS

Stairs
Stairway surfaces, like rostra, should be underlayed, to prevent resonance and inappropriate sound quality.

Obstruction
Hanging scenery can restrict the sound-boom operator's view, and can prevent free boom movement.

Further Reading

BRETZ, RUDY:
Techniques of Television Production. McGraw-Hill, New York.
A discussion of TV production equipment, including general TV staging approaches.

LEVIN, RICHARD:
Television by Design. Bodley Head, London.
An outline of TV staging methods, together with examples of actual televised productions.

MILLERSON, GERALD:
The Technique of Lighting for Television and Motion Pictures. Focal Press, London and Boston.
A study of lighting techniques, including full discussion of their influence and application to staging.

MILLERSON, GERALD:
The Technique of Television Production. Focal Press, London and Boston.
A comprehensive examination of TV production techniques, revealing their relationship to staging and design principles.

WADE, ROBERT J.:
Designing for Television. Pellegrini & Cudahy, New York.
A survey of TV design principles and applications.

WADE, ROBERT J.:
Staging Television Programmes and Commercials. Hastings House, New York.
Productional applications in network programmes and commercials, of TV staging.

WILKIE, BERNARD:
The Technique of Special Effects in Television. Focal Press, London and Boston.
A detailed exposition on methods of obtaining a wide range of visual effects; many of which directly relate to staging illusions.

MILLERSON, GERALD:
TV Lighting Methods. Focal Press, London and Boston.
An introduction to the principles of lighting for television.

WILKIE, BERNARD:
Creating Special Effects. Focal Press, London and Boston.

Glossary

Achromatic (Neutral) Neutral tonal values (white, greys, black), without distinct hue, lacking colour.

Act Drop (18) Theatrical term. A drape (often front stage) lowered between acts (usually to permit scenic changes).

Acting Area (Action area) (14) (86) The region within a setting in which performance takes place.

Additive Colour Mixing (120) With coloured *light* where one colour is added to another to produce a colour-light mixture, the process is termed additive mixing. The light primaries universally used are red, green and blue. Together they result in white light.

Ambient Light (152) General light spilling upon a surface, particularly illuminating shadow areas and reducing overall contrast. Especially refers to random light spilling on to a picture tube (receiver or TV monitor), thus degrading the image.

Aspect Ratio The relative proportions of the horizontal and vertical sides of the screen. The TV standard format is 4 : 3 (i.e. 1·33 :1).

Backlight (110) Light shining towards the camera (usually on to the rear of a subject) to define its outline, or to model it slightly round edges.

Barndoor (118) A metal fitting attached to the front of a lamp-housing, comprising four independently hinged adjustable metal flaps on a rotatable frame. This permits precise cut-off of the light beam.

Batten (126) A theatrical term for a narrow wooden board, or for a stage lighting trough usually suspended overhead.

Batting Down on Blacks Crushing the darkest tones in a picture to an even black, as when adjusting the video of a black background caption to obliterate uneven lighting (shading, fall-off), or uneven background tone. See **Sit** (110).

Black Level (110) Technical term for that part of the video waveform representing black in the picture.

Bloom (Burn out) (44) A surface reflecting excessive light relative to the limits of a camera system appears as a blank white undetailed area. This may stem from or be aggravated by highly reflecting surface finish, too light a tone, the wrong lighting angle, or excessive light intensity.

Border (88) A hung vertical plane used to prevent cameras seeing over the top of staging and shooting into lamps, etc.

Book Wing (80) A free-standing unit comprising two hinged flats.

Bridge A suspended gangway or tubular-scaffolding fixture, providing a position for following-spot operation, or for rigging lighting equipment.

Brightness (44) A term used to indicate the quantity of light perceived from the subject. A subjective impression, easily confused due to physical and psychological effects. (In USA may equate to *luminosity*.)

Burn Out See **Bloom.**

Camera Rehearsal The studio period during which the programme is checked by intermittent or continuous rehearsal with cameras, and relative aspects of shots, staging, sound, lighting and costume, examined.

Camera Tower (148) A scaffolding tower (e.g. 9-12 ft high, 9 ft square), upon which a camera can be positioned for high shots.

Centre Stage A position in the centre of the acting area.

Chiaroscuro The most familiar pictorial style, in which emphasis is upon conveying an impression of solidity and depth by tonal gradation, planar brightnesses, tonal separation and shadow formations.

Chroma See **Saturation.**

Colour Cast An overall colour bias in a system (which is most clearly visible when 'black and white' subjects are shown). All colours will be inaccurately reproduced due to this imbalance between the three colour primaries.

Compatible Picture (46) (110) (120) Colour television systems are particularly engineered to permit a colour transmission to be viewed on a standard monochrome receiver with minimum perceptible spurious pattern in the reproduced picture.

Contrast Range (110) (124) (Subject brightness range) The ratio of the lightest and darkest tones in a scene that a system can accommodate simultaneously, while still reproducing intermediate tones well. Also the range of tones in any scene being discussed.

Contrast Ratio (44) The relative 'brightness' of two tones being discussed, given as a luminance ratio.

Costing (12) The economic assessment of costing materials, effort, production man-hours, etc., relative to equipment, facilities, hire and labour costs.

Cross Shot (90) A camera viewpoint that is oblique to an action area, as opposed to a *frontal shot*, in which the camera is positioned straight on to the scene.

Crush Out (44) (110) (136) To cause similar tones to merge, e.g. dark greys become black, or very light greys reproduce as overall white. Modelling is considerably reduced in such tones.

Cut Cloth A suspended canvas scenic cloth with uneven edges (profiled), or cut-out (stencilled) for a particular purpose, such as window openings.

Cyan (120) A blue-green hue. Minus red (i.e. white light minus its red component).

Depth of Field (112) The range of distances over which a scene is acceptably sharp when focused at a given point. Depth of field becomes deeper with reduced lens aperture, with greater camera distances from the subject, and with wider lens angles. The term 'depth of focus' is often used erroneously.

166

Dipping (98) The process of lightly dyeing a material to reduce its reflectance or modify its hue, usually to bring it within the video limits of the system. Thus, white shirts, blouses, sheets, coats, dust covers and lace curtains, are invariably dipped before use.

Dolly A small wheeled platform supporting a tripod, extensible pillar, or movable jib arm, upon which the camera head and panning head are fitted, so providing the camera with mobility of position and height. It may require one, two or three operators in addition to the cameraman.

Downstage A position near the camera. Opposite from **Upstage**.

Dulling Spray (98) A wax spray, used to reduce the shine of a reflective surface. Anti-flare.

Fill light (Filler, fill-in) (128) A diffused light used to illuminate shadows and reduce contrast without itself suggesting a prevailing light direction.

Fire Flicker A flickering light effect simulating firelight, achieved by a stick of rag-strips, or a mechanism situated in front of a ground lamp.

Flies (80) Theatrical term. An area above stage into which scenery, scenic cloths, lighting equipment, etc., are raised by lines and held suspended out of sight of the audience.

Flood (118) The adjustment of a spotlight (luminaire) to produce maximum coverage or spread (typically 60°) of its hard, focused light. Also a type of lamp providing light over a wide area.

Floor Lamp (72) (122) A lamp fixed to an adjustable metal stand, often constructed with a hollow central tube in a castored tripod base.

Floor Wash (136) The process of removing water-soluble paints (by hand or mechanical scrubbers) that have been used to tone or decorate the studio floor surface for staging.

Free Perspective (56) An arrangement in which scenic depth is exaggerated by deliberately emphasised and distorted perspective.

Grey Scale (44) (46) (120) A continuous tonal wedge displaying progressive reflectance values from black, through dark grey, mid grey and light grey to white. A 10-step grey scale is widely used, each step being logarithmically related. Overall contrast is about 20:1.

Grid (40) A grid framework (e.g. of tubular scaffolding) near the studio roof, providing access to hoists, lighting and suspension. A ceiling grid may be used to support lamps, scenery, etc.

Heavy Gang The crew responsible for the movement of heavy staging and equipment for the transportation, handling, scenic erection and striking. Known also as stage hands, scene crew, servicing operatives.

Hoist (80) A remotely winched or motor-driven mechanism, controlling a ceiling-located wire cable used to support scenery, or suspend lighting equipment.

Hot (136) An over-bright area on a subject, causing it to appear unduly light to pale off, or to *bloom*. It may result from over-lighting (i.e. excessive light intensity), from over-exposure, from a surface tone that is too light, or from surface shine.

Hot Spot (136) An over-bright localised patch of light often due to specular reflection from a shiny surface. In rear projection, uneven illumination in which the centre of the screen image is brighter than its edges.

House Lights Powerful ceiling lights used to illuminate the studio overall for general working purposes (e.g. rigging staging). Extinguished when specific, controlled studio lighting equipment in use.

Hue (116) (120) The predominant sensation of colour, i.e. red, green, blue, etc. Normally corresponds to a narrow spectral band.

Intensity See **Saturation**.

Jelly A diffuser placed in front of a lamp to reduce light intensity and/or to soften the emergent light. Plastic medium positioned in front of a lamp to colour the emergent light.

Key Light The main lamp lighting a subject, usually a spotlight (a hard, shadow-producing light source) and normally positioned slightly above and to the side of the subject relative to the camera viewpoint.

Lens Angle (12) The horizontal angle of view of a given lens; its horizontal coverage of the scene. Vertical lens angle is three-quarters of its corresponding horizontal field. This fixed lens angle may be altered slightly by the addition of clip-on supplementary lenses. (A zoom lens has a variable lens angle with a range, perhaps, of 5° to 50°).

Lens Aperture (112) An adjustable diameter diaphragm within the lens housing, known variously as the lens stop, iris or diaphragm. Aperture change simultaneously alters the amount of light passed by lens (hence the *exposure*), and the depth of field.

Library Shots (Stock shot) (60) A film length (shot or sequence) classified as containing particular action, subject, location, etc. (e.g. aerial view of Sydney Harbour bridge). The general purpose film may be inserted into any programme requiring this illustration without recourse to specially shooting the subject for the programme.

Light Balance The process of adjusting the relative intensities of lamps to obtain a specific effect.

Lighting Setting The process of directing lamps, adjusting their precise angle and coverage, and arranging the light quality, colour and intensity to suit their individual purposes.

Lightness The perceived brightness of surface colour.

Limbo (16) (62) A neutral background to action—generally white. (Term sometimes used for totally black backgrounds, more widely termed *cameo.*)

Line Beating (Strobing) A rapid flickering effect due to a *moiré pattern* formation.

Live (14) Direct transmission of a programme as it happens, as opposed to one that has been video recorded or filmed.

Luminance The true measured brightness of a surface (doubling the illumination produces double the surface luminance). Snow has a high luminance, black velvet an extremely low luminance. (Not to be confused with the impression made on the eye—See **Brightness** and **Lightness**).

Luminosity The perceived brightness of a light source. (In USA *brightness* is often used instead.)

Magenta (120) A red-blue hue. Minus green (i.e. white light minus its green component).

Man Hours (12) The theoretical work-effect achieved by a man in one hour; a unit used in the calculation of manpower requirements, staffing, etc., for projects (e.g. construction or erection).

Marks (Floor marks) Small, L-shaped floor marks crayoned to indicate the position of chair feet, furniture, scenery, actors' positions (toe-marks), to ensure accuracy in repeated positioning.

Mask (88) Any surface positioned to prevent the camera from seeing a particular area. (Hence the verb 'to mask').

Mirror Ball (58) (116) A suspended, motor-rotated ball, surfaced with many small mirrors. Lit by a spotlight, numerous random points of light are reflect and traverse the scene.

Moiré Pattern A disturbance effect perceived in the picture, due to the near-coincidence of scenic pattern, and the TV scanning lines, creating a mesh pattern (often *line beating*). Particularly evident in close shots of engravings, close horizontal lines, and checked tweeds.

Monitor Tube A small oscilloscope used to display a graphical representation of the video waveform, to enable video equipment performance to be maintained within specified limits.

Munsell Scale (158) A system of colour notation, in which pages of sample chips methodically analyse progressively varied hues. Each hue is displayed at varying saturation (chroma) and luminance (value), thereby permitting each aspect to be numerically classified.

Narrow Angle Lens (86) A camera lens with a narrow angle of view—e.g. less than 10°. The viewed picture appears to contain compressed perspective, so that the effects of space and distance are reduced, depth and thickness are decreased. Contouring is flattened.

Notan (156) A pictorial style directing attention to outline, surface colour and detail, but not concerned with the solid form of the subject.

O/P Side (Opposite prompt) The left hand side of the stage (viewed from audience and camera position).

Off Stage A position outside the acting area. To move 'off stage' is to move away from the centre of an acting area.

On Stage A position inside the acting area. To move 'on stage' is to move more towards the centre of an acting area.

Over-Exposed A picture in which lightest tones are unmodelled and darkest tones may appear over-light. All picture tones are generally lightened, including faces, which appear pale.

Overnight Set The erection of staging (and floor painting) carried out overnight (after lighting rigging) in readiness for the setting lighting and for subsequent camera rehearsal.

Pedestal (Electronic). An element of the transmitted TV signal; a deliberately increased black level limit.
(Camera). A type of highly mobile, three-wheeled camera mounting with a central column of rapidly-adjustable height (hydraulic, pneumatic, or spring-controlled for fingertip movement). Operated entirely by one cameraman.

Perch A platform built to one side of a stage, close to the proscenium arch.

Picture Monitor High-grade TV picture display for monitoring (assessment) purposes. It may show a selected video source (e.g. a particular camera's output), or switch between several sources. The picture monitor does not include a sound system (provided by a separate audio channel), and is not designed for off-air reception.

Picture Tube The cathode ray tube (CRT) in a TV receiver or monitor upon the face of which the TV picture is displayed.

Plumbicon A type of TV camera pick-up tube developed from the Vidicon, especially for use in colour TV cameras. A lightweight, stable tube, but possessing some problems in lag, and less sensitivity to red.

Practical (102) (104) (158) Working (e.g. a table-lamp that lights). Hence *non-practical*, means ornamental or not required to function (the item may be broken, or simply not made operational). *Fully practical* indicates that an item that is normally used only decoratively as scenic dressing must be completely working (e.g. a tape recorder).

Prompt Side The right hand side of the stage (viewed from audience and camera position).

Properties (Props.) (98) The various scenic articles used to decorate a setting, including those to be handled by performers. *Personal props* are items specifically used or worn by a particular actor or character (such

as spectacles or a wallet). *Action props.* include items used in the course of action, such as a coffee pot or newspaper.
Purity See **Saturation**.

Rake Slope of a floor.
Recording Break (14) A pause in a recording session during which recording ceases, and essential studio changes take place (make-up and costume, scenery, set dressing, lighting, etc., altered).
Reflectance (44) The proportion of light reflected from a surface is designated its reflectance. Total reflection from a surface of 100% reflectance; no reflectance from a surface that has 0% reflectance (i.e. 100% absorption). Fresh snow = 93 to 97% reflectance. Black velvet = 0·3 to 1% reflectance. In fact, reflectance will vary with the colour of the incident light, and surface texture, surface colour and tone.
Re-Take (14) To re-enact action and production operations, usually to rectify or improve some technical, operational, or performance aspect of the production during videorecording.
Rig To set up, install; especially relative to rigging lamps (also slung microphones, loudspeakers and picture monitors).

Safety Bond A clipped metal or wire strop attached to equipment or scenery to ensure its stability, hold it erect, prevent portions falling off, etc.
Saturation (Chroma, intensity, purity) The extent to which colour has been 'diluted' (paled or greyed-off) by the addition of white light. 100% saturation represents the pure, undiluted colour.
Scene Dock Scenic storage area, often adjacent to the studio.
Set Down See **Sit** (110).
Shade A pure hue mixed with black, darkening it.
Shot (14) The basic production unit. The picture sequence from a single camera, between two transitions (i.e. cut, mix, etc.). Also, designates a specific camera set-up with reference to position, image size, height, long shot, close shot, etc.
Silhouette (116) (156) A pictorial style concentrating entirely upon subject outline, completely obliterating colour, tone, texture and modelling.
Sit (110) Electrical adjustment of the video waveform (its D.C. component) to move all picture tones down (or up) the tonal scale, the effect being most noticeable in darker values. (See **Batting Down on Blacks**.)
Skid A roller-mechanism traversing a weight-carrying ceiling joist or girder, and supporting a rope and tackle or wire cable. The rope or cable is used to support scenery, to suspend lights, equipment, etc.
Special Effects Department of specialists responsible for the creation

of harmless and economic illusions suggesting catastrophies, fire, destruction, as well as creating and operating the 'impossible', such as monsters and gimmick apparatus.

Spot (118) (140) General term for a spotlight; a light-source providing a hard, sharply focused beam. Also, adjustment of a fresnel spotlight for minimum coverage (about 10°) and, hence, maximum intensity. (*Follow-spot* is a more specialised unit used to produce a localised disc of light, such as that used to illuminate a soloist).

Staging Area (126) The main area of the studio floor, within which staging can be arranged. Indicated on the studio plan by a scaled grid, it is surrounded by a safety area (fire lane) in which staging is normally prohibited.

Stock Shot See **Library Shot** (60).

Stop, Lens (112) Lens diaphragms are graduated in theoretical units called *stops* or *f-numbers*, indicating the relative light-passing properties of the lens system at each setting. (T-numbers, show true light transmission difference.)

Streaking (44) (102) (136) Picture defect in which spurious horizontal bars spread across a picture from high contrast scenic areas.

Strike (20) (80) To dismantle scenery.

Subtractive Colour Mixing (120) Surface colour derives from the absorption of light. Each coloured pigment absorbs (subtracts) its own section of the spectrum. Hence, by mixing the pigment colour primaries, magenta, yellow, cyan, the subtractive combination results in a black surface reflecting little light.

Teaser (88) A plane surface hung over the set to prevent shoot-off.

Tint A pure hue diluted with white making it more pale.

Tone (158) A pure hue diluted with grey.

Top Light ('Toppy') (158) Light directed on to a subject from above or from an extremely steep vertical angle. A very undesirable practice, producing crude facial modelling, bright tops to heads, etc.

Tormentor Theatrical term. A flat located at the side of a stage near the proscenium arch, for masking purposes.

Trailer Drapes Background drapes that open and close on a horizontal track.

Trailing (Lag effect) (136) A picture defect in which an ectoplasmic smear persists behind a moving subject.

Traveler (32) A drape suspended from an overhead track, that may be drawn to one side by a pulley mechanism.

Turret A fitting on monochrome TV cameras in which a selection of three or four lenses of differing angles is held in a rotatable disc (turret) at the front of the damera head. The chosen lens can be moved into position for shooting, and is termed the 'taking lens'.

Under-Exposed A picture in which all scenic tones are darkened. General symptoms include poor shadow gradation, insufficient visibility in lower tones, over-dark faces. It is due to too small a lens aperture (stop), or to insufficient light intensities.

Upstage (158) Strictly speaking, a position towards the back wall of a setting. Often used to indicate a position far from the camera. Hence 'move upstage' indicates to move away from a particular camera.

Value (44) A classification used by the Munsell system to denote apparent, subjective brightness (i.e. that seen by the eye, which has a logarithmic sensitivity).

Video Tape (14) (20) A video recording system using magnetic tape. Monochromatic or colour pictures can be permanently recorded. The resultant record can be demagnetised, completely or in segments, as required, and the tape material re-used many times. Editing is readily achieved by re-recording processes, or sometimes by cutting and splicing.

Vidicon A type of TV camera pick-up tube. Widely used in smaller monochrome studios, and in industrial applications. (Susceptible to picture lag.)

Wide Angle Lens (88) A camera lens with a wide angle of view (over 45°). The viewed picture appears to contain exaggerated perspective, so that space and distance are emphasised and depth and thickness look greater than normal. Contouring is enhanced.

Wind Machine (142) (160) An electric fan mechanism of adjustable speed used to simulate wind effects. (Very liable to produce loud rumbling noises as the wind strikes microphones in the area.)

Working Light Any light introduced to enable craftsmen, performers or others to see what they are doing when other lighting in the vicinity has been extinguished.

Zoom Lens (132) A specially designed lens system that permits the *lens angle* to be continually adjusted from narrow to wide angle settings, and held at any intermediate chosen coverage. See **Turret**.